May

Dear John,

Congratulations on finishing eighteen years of education. I regret having missed the first seventeen and a half. Thanks for the sympathetic ear, the shoulder to lean on, the cigarettes, for putting up with the euphemisms and cat stories, but most of all, thanks for caring. Good luck!

Love,

Chris

Cats and Kittens

Cats and Kittens

Howard Loxton

Exeter Books
NEW YORK

Photographic acknowledgments

Animal Photography – Michael Crawley 93; Animal Photography – Sally Anne Thompson 13 bottom, 20 bottom, 23, 24 bottom, 26 bottom, 29, 36, 37, 38 bottom, 39 top, 39 bottom, 40 top, 41, 42, 43 top, 46, 47, 50 top, 50 bottom, 52 top, 54 top, 55 top, 55 bottom, 64, 65, 66 top, 68 top, 73 top, 73 bottom, 78 top, 78 bottom, 79, 81, 88, 90–91, 105, 112, 113, 115, 116, 126, 127; Ardea 6, 7, 8 top, 9 top, 9 bottom, 25, 26 top, 38 top, 46, 53, 58, 59, 70 top, 71, 74, 76, 96, 119; BBC Hulton Picture Library 19; Bruce Coleman 56 bottom; Cats' Protection League 24 top; Colour Library International 10 bottom, 12, 13 top, 14, 15 top, 21, 22 top, 22 bottom, 30, 34–35, 48, 57, 75, 80, 82 top, 83, 84–85, 86 top, 110, 111, 117, 120; Mary Evans Picture Library 18, 20 top; Hamlyn Group Picture Library 28, 33, 40 bottom, 51 top, 51 bottom, 52 bottom, 54 bottom, 56 top, 60, 66 bottom, 67, 95, 97, 99, 100, 101, 109 bottom; Michael Holford 16, 17 left, 17 right; Eric Inglefield 128; Howard Loxton 104 bottom, 106, 107; Natural History Photographic Agency 8 bottom, 27, 124; Spectrum Colour Library 10 top, 15 bottom, 31, 44 top, 70 bottom, 82 bottom, 86 bottom, 87 left, 87 right, 89, 91 bottom, 92, 94, 98, 103, 104 top, 108, 109 top, 121, 122, 123, 125; Zefa 32, 43 bottom, 49, 69 bottom, 77, 84 top, 114, 118.

Front cover: Sally Anne Thompson
Back cover: Colour Library International
Title page: Sally Anne Thompson

First published in USA 1984
by Exeter Books
Distributed by Bookthrift
Exeter is a trademark of Simon & Schuster
Bookthrift is a registered trademark of Simon & Schuster
New York, New York

Prepared by
Deans International Publishing
52–54 Southwark Street, London SE1 1UA
A division of The Hamlyn Publishing Group Limited
London · New York · Sydney · Toronto

ISBN 0-671-06906-3

Printed and bound by Graficromo s.a., Córdoba, Spain

Contents

The Tiger on the Hearth

The cat is one of the most recent animals to have been domesticated by man but it belongs to a family of animals that evolved long before the appearance of *homo sapiens*. Fossil records show that about fifty million years ago there was a weasel-like carnivorous mammal with a long body and short legs, which has been given the name *Miacis*. From it appear to have developed a whole range of animals: the racoon, civet, mongoose, bear, hyena, wolf, otter, skunk, dog – and the cat. About forty million years ago one of its descendants was recognizably a form of cat – it was about another ten million before a form of dog appeared.

This first cat, known as *Dinictis*, was about the size of a modern lynx but had a much smaller brain than modern cats and much larger canine teeth (the long, fang-like teeth on either side of the central incisors). From *Dinictis* feline evolution went in two separate directions. On the one hand the canine teeth became even larger to pro-

Right: Leopards, like domestic cats, are good at climbing trees. They often haul their kill up into the branches so that other predators do not steal it.

Below: The Cheetah is the fastest of all mammals. It can reach speeds of 60 mph (100 kmh).

duce big cats, including a genus called *Machairodus* (although some palaeontologists think that *Dinictis* should actually be classed in the same group as this animal). The other branch, with smaller canine teeth, included the *Felidae*, the group to which all the modern cats belong.

In southern California, not far from San Francisco, are the Rancho La Brea asphalt pits. Here, back in the Pleistocene times, numerous animals and birds became trapped in soft tar, and their bones were preserved in the asphalt. One of the most numerous animals preserved was *Smilodon californicus*, an advanced New World sabre-tooth, whose long canine teeth curved well beyond the lower jaw when its mouth was closed and could not be used for biting but probably delivered a violent stabbing blow. These sabre-tooths became extinct about 13,000 years ago but in Europe sabre-tooths disappeared much earlier. Also in the tar pits, and contemporary with *Smilodon*, were the bones of a big cat four times larger than the modern lion called *Panthera atrox*, whose close relation in the Old World, *Panthera leo spelaea*, is thought to have survived in northern Greece until about 500 BC.

Even the biggest members of the cat family that survive today are comparatively small compared with those ancient creatures but they probably do not differ greatly in their anatomy and way of life. All the thirty-two different species of big and little cats, from the lion and tiger, snow leopard and jaguar to the small spotted cats of Asia and the wild cats of Africa and Europe, have immediately identifiable cat-like qualities. So alike are they that zoologists cannot come to a firm agreement about their taxonomy. Some say that they should almost all be placed in a single genus, *Felis*; others that the differences between the big cats and the smaller cats are enough to warrant two: *Felis* and *Panthera*. They all agree that the cheetah, *Acinonyx jubatus*, stands on its own – although its main difference is that its claws are not retracted fully into its paws once it develops beyond early kittenhood. The lion, tiger, leopard, clouded leopard, snow leopard and jaguar have all been placed in the separate genus, *Panthera*, because they lack a bone at the base of the tongue, having instead only a thread-like ligament so that the tongue is but loosely attached to the base of the

Right: Most of the cat family tend to live and hunt alone but lions live in family groups, called prides, the females being responsible for most of the hunting.

Below: The puma used to range over the whole of the Americas from Alaska to Cape Horn, living in pine forest, prairie and jungle. In North America hunting and the spread of agriculture now restrict it mainly to National Parks and reserves.

skull. The big cats can roar, the smaller cats cannot, and the smaller cats can maintain a continuous purr, whereas the big ones have to take a breath between each purr. Those are the differences which the taxonomists draw between the big cat and the tiger on your hearth.

What was the wild origin of the domestic cat? Most opinion favours the African Wildcat, *Felis lybica*, although the European Wildcat, *Felis sylvestris*, is almost identical – some people think they should be classed as the same species. Both can breed with the domestic cat. The European Wildcat looks like a very heavily built tabby. It has a larger skull and teeth and its fur is somewhat longer than shorthaired domestic pets, but the easiest way to distinguish it from domestic cats is by its rather short, bushy and rounded tail. At one time it was quite common throughout woodland territory from Britain (not Ireland) across to Western Asia, but it has now retreated to areas away from man, such as the more remote parts of Scotland. In its African form the Wildcat shows considerable variation in coat and seems the most likely origin for the first domestic cats of which we have positive evidence: the pets of ancient

Top: The Wildcat looks like a heavily built domestic cat, and is probably its closest relative. It often has tabby markings.

Above: The Jungle Cat, larger and more lithe looking than the African Wildcat, may also have been an ancestor of the domestic cat.

Egypt. It is comparatively easy to tame – the European Wildcat is not – and a study of 192 Egyptian mummified cats in the British Museum showed that most were *Felis lybica*, four were the slightly larger Jungle Cat, *Felis chaus*, and the rest were a half-way stage between the African Wildcat and the modern domestic cat. Elsewhere such species as the Rusty-spotted cat, *Felis rubiginosus*, of southern India and Sri Lanka, also may have played a part in the ancestry of the domestic cat.

All cats are carnivores, although this does not mean that they never eat vegetation, and their bodies have developed into highly efficient hunting machines. Their skeletons do not appear to be very different from our own except that we have lost our tails and that the cat walks on its paws, which are the equivalent of our fingers and toes. However, there are other differences. A cat's spine, for instance, is much more pliable than ours, enabling the animal to bend and arch its back more; its limbs are extremely flexible – its forelegs can be moved in almost any direction; and its head can be turned much further to the rear than ours. Look at a cat washing itself and think how difficult it would be for you to get into the positions that it can adopt. This very versatile frame is controlled by powerful muscles which are especially strong in the area of the pelvis and hind legs, giving it a powerful spring, and in the neck and shoulders, which come into use when striking prey. These muscles can take a great deal of strain but the cat's heart and lungs cannot. Because finding and catching prey is unpredictable and there may be long gaps between one successful kill and the next the cat has to be able to cope with occasional feasts and sometimes long gaps between one meal and the next. That means that it has to have a comparatively large stomach and digestive system, so that it can eat a great deal and then absorb it slowly, which leaves less space for the heart and lungs. A cat's breathing and pulse rate are much faster than ours and although it can produce great bursts of energy it cannot sustain them. Take a cat for even a leisurely walk and it will tire within half an hour, as Konrad Lorenz pointed out. Its pattern is one of spasmodic activity interspersed with pauses to recover.

A cat's teeth are a vital part of its equipment. They are typical carnivore teeth – none of them has much grinding power. The central incisors in both jaws are very small

some other orientals the claws do not get drawn so far back into the paw and when they are walking on a smooth surface, such as a polished floor, you can hear a sharp click as they touch although they will not protrude so that they scratch unless the cat wishes them to do so.

The cat has a well-developed brain, much the same as ours except that we have larger frontal lobes, memory association areas and a speech centre. It has a complex limbic system – the emotional centre – so a cat probably experiences much the same emotions as we do, and its motor control and sensory appraisal are well developed. In some respects its senses are more highly developed than our own.

Cats locate their prey by sight and sound and both their eyes and their ears are very sensitive. Their eyes are large, compared with the size of the skull, and placed well forward so that they cover the same field of view and give stereoscopic vision (animals with eyes

but very sharp. On either side in each jaw are two large canines, which can rip, tear, stab and grip, and are used both in fighting and feeding, and beyond them sharp-pointed serrated molars which chop up food into small pieces.

Claws are the other feature in the feline armoury but they are not just weapons, they help to keep a grip on slippery surfaces and enable a cat climb a tree or to find a hold when running up a wall. The front claws are wickedly pointed, regularly shedding their outer covering to reveal a newly-sharp point, and used for tearing food, fighting and often for gently picking things up. The hind claws are not so sharp or so curved but with the strong hind legs can strike a vicious blow when fighting. Cats' claws are retractable and when they are drawn back into the sheath the paw offers a soft and gentle surface. In adult Siamese cats and

Opposite, top: The cat has a formidable array of sharp teeth. Its tongue is covered with raised papillae which help to scrape meat off bones and form a scrubbing brush and comb when grooming. The number of ridges on a cat's mouth used to be thought to show how good a mouser it would be.

Opposite, below: A layer of reflecting cells at the back of a cat's eyes helps to make it see better in poor light and produces the red-eyed effect of the cat on the right.

Below: In bright light, like the glare of a photographer's photo-floods, the iris of a cat's eye shrinks to a narrow slit.

that look to each side see two separate images). This enables them to judge distance and they are usually very good at doing so, especially when leaping. Each eye can see through an angle of over 200° and, since they can turn their necks so far round, they can scan a very wide area with little movement. Cats' eyes are not as responsive to colour as our eyes, having only about one fifth of the proportion of colour cells, and they also seem less able to distinguish stationary objects or to focus at close quarters – but they can see through a great range of light intensities. In bright light the pupil, or iris, of the eye closes up to a narrow vertical slit, cutting down the amount of light entering. In dim light it opens up to a full circle and when light passes through the eye it strikes a triangular area at the rear of the eye's upper part, known as the *tapetum lucidum*, in which the retinal cells are backed by cells which act like a mirror, reflecting much of the light back through the eye to repeat its sensory message on the retina. When you see a cat's eyes shining in the darkness it is that reflected light that you see. It usually looks red, the other parts of

the spectrum presumably having been absorbed. Other nocturnal animals also have this intensification system but we do not and consequently the cat can see in light so dim that we would probably consider it to be pitch dark. To protect the eye from dazzlingly bright light and from damage in a fight or when pushing through undergrowth the cat also has a supplementary eyelid, the haw or nictitating membrane, a translucent piece of skin which lies in the inner corner of the eye and can be drawn upwards across it. It also helps to clean the eye. If a cat is ill the haw will often stay partially raised and this is a useful, but not infallible, indication that it is off colour. It can occur sometimes in healthy animals, particularly it is said, if they have been eating grasshoppers!

When it becomes too dark for even a cat to see its other senses must take over. Perhaps you have walked through a very dark room and felt that you could actually sense where furniture or other obstacles were placed. In a cat this sensitivity is highly developed. It has often been said that a cat's whiskers enable it to judge the width of spaces to see if it can get its body through – and there is some truth in this, not, as is often thought, because their extent matches its body width, but because the whiskers are part of the cat's touch system. The long hairs called vibrissae (whiskers, eyebrows, hairs on the back of the forepaws) and pressure sensitive spots all over a cat's body transmit messages back to the brain, not just of things that they actually touch but also of pressure changes in the air caused by the presence of objects. The front paws are very touch sensitive (like our fingertips) and you will often see a cat investigating with them and with the tip of its nose, which is also very sensitive. Even the gentlest touch on a cat's spine will produce a strong reaction, if it is unexpected, but cats also seem to get great pleasure from touch and physical contact – there does not seem to be a single cat that does not like being stroked, whether it is a mongrel or a pedigree.

Hearing is often used by cats to locate an object, not only in the dark but also to provide a fix for their eyes to pick it out. You can see a cat moving its ears to focus on a sound; they are contoured and ridged to concentrate the sound waves and highly manoeuvrable. By contrast with human beings cats can hear over a wide range of sound – from 30 to 45,000 hertz or higher. Our top limit is around 20,000 hertz and, except for very low notes, cats can hear better than us even in our optimum range. Throw a piece of crumpled paper and a cat will place its position exactly, although it has not seen it land, and any cat owner will know that their pet will recognize the footsteps of a friend or the motor of a car long before a human's ears can even hear them.

The cat's ears also play an important part in its incredible sense of balance. While many people and dogs suffer from travel sickness, on boats or in cars, it seems that cats seldom do. It is possible that a cat's inner ear is different in some way not yet understood. Cats can also manage

Above: A cat's eyebrows and whiskers are part of its sensitive touch system.

Left: The nictitating membrane may be rising from the corner of this kitten's eyes to cut out bright light or dust, but its appearance often indicates that a cat is not well.

Right: A cat's almost perfect sense of balance enables it to traverse the narrow top of a fence. Note that the claws are extended on one hind foot to gain purchase, but retracted on the front paw until needed.

to right themselves when falling so that they land on their feet – although since deaf cats (and even one born without any inner ear) are able to do this it cannot be entirely dependent upon the ear structure. However, it should not be assumed that because they can do this they never hurt themselves! Falls from very short distances may not give them time to turn, and falls from great heights may lead to damage because of the force of the fall, even though the righting mechanism works. A cat that is not properly awake may also fail to right itself and for this reason cats should be discouraged from napping on outside upstairs window ledges unless there is some sort of barrier to stop them slipping off if they turn in their sleep.

Smell is not as important to cats as it is to many other animals, who use it to track down their prey, but it is a major way of identifying both animals and objects and the sense is highly developed in the cat. A new-born kitten finds its way to its mother's nipples by scent – its eyes do not open until about eight days later – and scent carries the message that there is a potential mate in the neighbourhood to local toms, or a strange cat in another cat's territory, and it is an important way of distinguishing friends. Cats seem to delight in smells: they will open their mouths wide, to permit as much air as possible to enter, and draw it up into two ducts, placed in the hard palate behind the upper incisors, which lead to a smell organ supplementary to the nose. A cat will often sit by an open window open-mouthed, savouring the symphony of smells that wafts in from outside or sniff in the odour from some pungent object (often a smell that humans find distasteful, although cats also like conventional perfumes). When someone arrives home the cat will sniff feet and clothes to see where they (or another animal) have been and will use its nose to check out all the goodies in a bag of shopping. For cats the succession of smell sensations is rather like you giving a detailed account of everywhere you have been and everything you have done – or showing a friend a set of snapshots of your travels.

For most animals, scent messages – pheromones – are a vital part of life and are quite positively deposited. An adult male cat spraying urine near his home is claiming the area as his home territory and warning other tom-cats that it is occupied. In areas where there is no territorial competition – or where there are so many cats that territories become restricted to very small areas – it may perhaps be treated as a calling card, like someone chalking on a wall 'Kilroy was here'. In the same way, a cat that rubs its head and body against your legs is not just being friendly or asking for attention. It is actually leaving a scent message saying this is my friend, and perhaps implying that he is not prepared to share you with every Ginger, Fluffy or Tiger. The head rub, and probably the tail rub too, brings contact with scent-producing glands which are abundant on each side of the forehead, are placed along the tail and also occur on the lips and chin.

It has been suggested that cats do not have a highly developed sense of taste. Owners whose pets are faddy about foods will probably disagree, although texture, smell and other features will also be important in making them like a food. Taste perception varies greatly among humans, perhaps it does in cats. Some appear to have no discrimination, others a great deal, though adult cats seem generally not to be so responsive to sweet things and their sensitivity gets stronger through salt, bitter and sour tastes.

Cats also have an uncanny sense of time, knowing exactly when to expect someone home, for instance. And many have shown an amazing talent for finding their way home, or even for finding a new home to which their human friends have moved.

Opposite, top: A cat will twist its body as it falls so that it can make a four-footed landing.

Above: What is it about these maple leaves that smells so wonderful? Cats seem to get great pleasure from their sense of smell.

Right: A cat rubbing against you is not just saying 'Hello'. It is probably leaving a scent message too. Its forehead will usually make contact first, then the body and finally the tail curling round your legs.

The History of the Cat

When did the cat first become domesticated? It was certainly long after the dog had become man's companion and after the husbandry of animals had begun. Although cat bones have been found in association with prehistoric man in Switzerland and one cat was discovered with finds of 2000 BC in the Indus Valley there is no evidence that these were domesticated – or even that the earliest cats seen in Egyptian wall paintings were not wild animals. What is certain is that the cat became an important part of Egyptian culture.

A wall painting from a Theban tomb of 1400 BC shows a wildfowler and a cat out hunting.

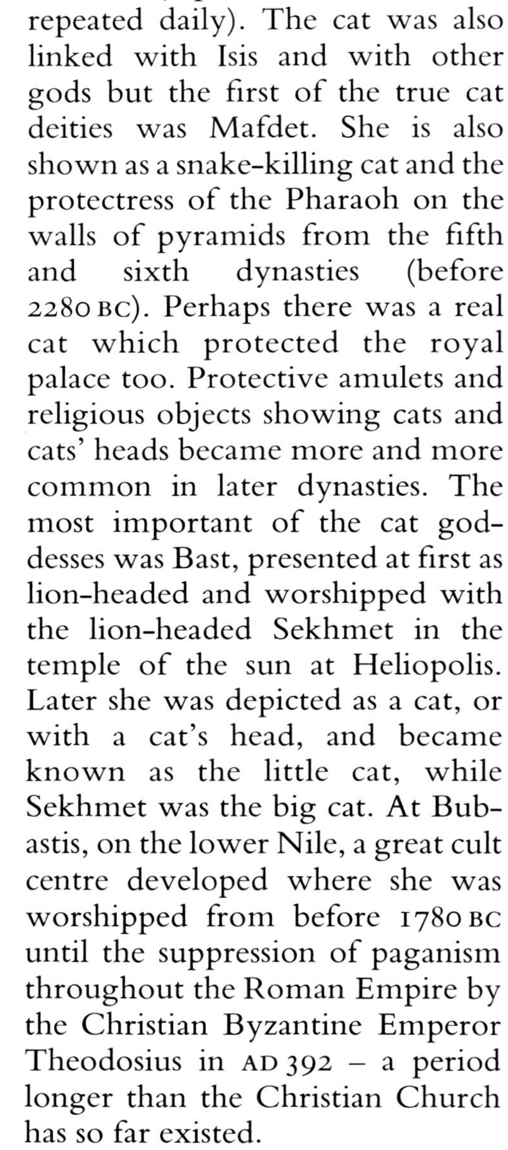

The cat was one form taken by the great sun god Ra, who is shown in cat form defeating the serpent of darkness (a process that had to be repeated daily). The cat was also linked with Isis and with other gods but the first of the true cat deities was Mafdet. She is also shown as a snake-killing cat and the protectress of the Pharaoh on the walls of pyramids from the fifth and sixth dynasties (before 2280 BC). Perhaps there was a real cat which protected the royal palace too. Protective amulets and religious objects showing cats and cats' heads became more and more common in later dynasties. The most important of the cat goddesses was Bast, presented at first as lion-headed and worshipped with the lion-headed Sekhmet in the temple of the sun at Heliopolis. Later she was depicted as a cat, or with a cat's head, and became known as the little cat, while Sekhmet was the big cat. At Bubastis, on the lower Nile, a great cult centre developed where she was worshipped from before 1780 BC until the suppression of paganism throughout the Roman Empire by the Christian Byzantine Emperor Theodosius in AD 392 – a period longer than the Christian Church has so far existed.

In the courtyard of the temple at Bubastis priests watched the temple cats for any sign in their behaviour that might be a message from the goddess and every year thousands of people came down

Left: *A bronze figure of Bast, shown in human form with a cat's head and attendant cats. She is holding an aegis, a form of purse, embellished with a cat's head carrying the disc of the sun, and shakes a sistrum, a metal rattle.*

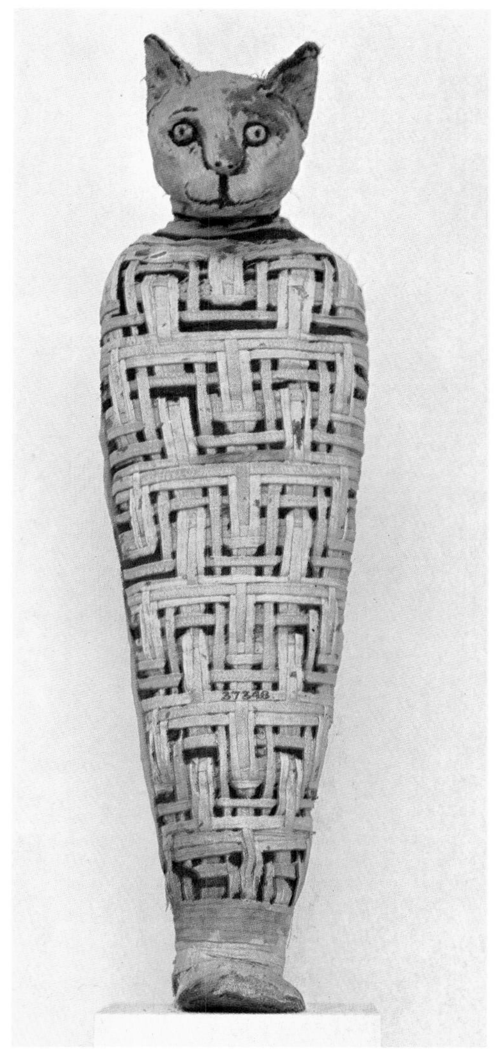

Above: *Treated with chemicals, wrapped in bandages and then in this intricately interwoven covering, decorated with paint or embroidery, Egyptian cats were mummified just like their owners.*

the river in decorated boats for an orgiastic festival in her honour. Nearby, at Beni Hassan, extensive catacombs were excavated in which more than 30,000 mummified cats were discovered, revered pets sent here for burial from all over Egypt.

Wall paintings and papyri, and faience and bronze figures often depict cats. Several wall paintings show them out with wildfowlers hunting in the reed beds of the Nile delta. The cats were probably used to flush out the water birds and may perhaps have been trained to retrieve the birds knocked down by the throwing stick seen in the hunters' hands.

Egyptian law forbade the export of cats, which suggests that they saw the domestic animal as something distinctly different from the wild cat species, but nevertheless they found their way to other countries. The Greeks do not seem

to have set great store by them, although pet cats do appear in some vase paintings and a carved statue base from around 500 BC shows a cat and a dog on leads. The Romans gave the cat rather more attention, although it was not until the fourth century AD that an agricultural author recommended them for rodent control. They were taken up much earlier as an exotic pet, along with the fashion for Egyptian religions. The Romans probably took cats to the furthest parts of the empire – skeletons have been found, for instance, in Roman villas in Britain, although it is possible that the cat may have reached the British Isles earlier with the Phoenicians who traded between Egypt and the tin mines of Cornwall.

It was not only the Egyptian and Romano-Egyptian religions that found a place for cats. The Chinese had an agricultural god in cat form and cats were linked with Nordic goddesses, while in the New World Peruvians had a cat-like fertility god and other members of the cat family featured in both the Aztec and Inca religions.

The Romans had linked the goddess Bast with their goddess

Above: In Egypt harming a cat was a serious crime and when a household cat died the whole family shaved off their eyebrows in mourning.

Opposite, top: In Europe in the Middle Ages the cat was associated with witches and the devil. An engraving by Hans Baldung (1476–1545).

Diana (the Greek Artemis), goddess of hunting and the moon, and thus the cat came to be identified with Hecate, queen of witches. To the Christian Church the cat was pagan and seen as closely associated with the devil. Medieval Breton peasants used to believe that the cat slept through the day so that it might act as watchman during the night, warning the devil's spirits of the approach of any intruder – the noise of scurrying vermin in the straw being thought to be the sound of spirits hurrying away.

Followers of the Albigensian and Waldesian sects, tried and tortured for heresy by the Roman Church, 'confessed' to carrying out rites involving cats and early in the fourteenth century Knights Templar, tortured when Pope Clement V decided to suppress the order, admitted to worshipping the devil in the shape of a black tom-cat. In Metz, France, in 1344, the appearance of the devil as a black cat was said to have caused an outbreak of St Vitus' dance.

As late as the end of the fifteenth century Pope Innocent VII issued instructions for the Inquisition to seek out cat worshippers and through many centuries cats were persecuted. In Metz thirteen cats were burned each year in the town square and in Paris, Luxembourg and other cities similar barbaric bonfires were lit. By its persecution of the cat the Christian Church enabled the rat to flourish and through the Middle Ages wave after wave of plague spread through Europe.

This felinophobia was by no means universal. In Saxony the ninth-century ruler Henry I decreed that anyone who killed an adult cat should be fined sixty bushels of corn. A century later various legal systems in Wales also placed high value on the cat. One Welsh legal code valued a cat in the king's service as being of the same value as a milch sheep and its lamb and her wool together.

Nor were all Churchmen so set against the cat as the Popes mentioned. When the sixth-century Pope Gregory I retired to monastic life he chose a cat as his sole companion, and it was the only companion permitted to anchoresses of the Cistercian order. One Irish monk, spending his life copying manuscripts in a monastery during the nine or tenth century, wrote a delightful Latin poem about the cat who shared his cell:

I and Pangur Ban, my cat,
'Tis a like task we are at;
Hunting mice is his delight,
Hunting words I sit all night . . .

Later and grander clerics also cared for cats. Pope Leo XII had a greyish-red cat with black stripes, called Micetto, which was brought up in the folds of his robes; Cardinal Wolsey had a cat which went to services with him and Cardinal Richelieu had at least fourteen cats – though sadly, after Richelieu's death, Swiss mercenaries who thought the cardinal their enemy took revenge by killing them all.

To others, however, the Christian persecution caused great suffering – and not just to cats. In Europe thousands of men, women

Left: In England and North America great witch-hunts took place in the seventeenth century. Witches were often thought to have 'familiars', devil servants who took animal form, like these cats.
Below: Ships' cats are generally thought to bring good luck. This one is in Hong Kong harbour. Its owner seems determined not to let it run off and take its luck away.
Opposite, below: Judging the Siamese at a major British cat show. In Britain pens must not be decorated because judges visit them. In America the cats go to the judges, so prizes and colourful dressings can be displayed on the pens.

and children were tortured and killed – often by being burned at the stake – as witches. Both the Roman Catholic and the Protestant Churches hunted them. As well as believing that witches might worship the devil in cat form, they also thought that they could turn themselves into animals, including cats. One Scottish woman who confessed to being a witch in 1662 claimed that she could turn herself into a cat.

British witches were not burned – although they might have been hanged or drowned, and although people were accused of witchcraft from time to time the great witch-hunts did not begin in Britain until the end of the sixteenth century and the beginning of the seventeenth. James VI of Scotland, before he also became James I of England, was fascinated by witchcraft and wrote a book about it: *Daemonologie*.

In Europe it was believed that witches might have a devil as a supernatural servant, who also acted as their keeper, but the idea of a 'familiar', a servant in animal form, seems to have been a particularly British concept. Usually it was a small animal, a cat, dog or toad perhaps, for despite modern ideas of witches' cats the cat was not the most common animal, although there were many cases where a cat was named. Any household pet was likely to draw attention to someone who had upset part of the community and draw the witch-hunters to him or her for, as one Puritan parson who published a series of sermons on witchcraft in 1646 remarked, 'Every old woman with a wrinkled face, a hairy lip, a squint eye, a spindle in her hand, and a cat or dog by her side, is not only suspected but pronounced a witch.'

This realistic view was published at a time when Matthew Hopkins, the self-appointed 'Witch-finder General of England' had in two years sent more than 200 witches to their deaths.

The persecution crossed the Atlantic, encouraged by the publication of a book on witchcraft by Cotton Mather, a Puritan divine. The most famous North American trials were at Salem, Massachusetts, in 1692.

Back in Scotland, as late as 1718, a William Montgomery of Caithness claimed that hordes of cats gathered around his house speaking like people. One night he killed two with a hatchet and wounded others. Next day two old women were found dead and another had a wound on her leg which she could not explain. He was convinced that they had been witches in cat shape. Similar stories come from other parts of the world: from Norway for instance, and from the Ozark Mountains in Arkansas, where a man fired a pistol at an enormous cat and heard a woman's scream. In the morning he was told of a woman who had shot her foot off and died from loss of blood.

From Japan, too, come stories of witch cats and cat witches. One tells of a vampire cat which killed a prince's favourite lady and then assumed her form to take her place. If in Japan you see a cat that has two tails then you can be sure that it is a devil cat. But not all Japanese tales are of evil cats. One story tells of a cat which made the poor temple where she guarded sacred manuscripts become rich by taking all the travellers who passed along the road to make offerings there. All over Japan you may find a figure of a cat with a paw raised – the Maneki-neko, or beckoning cat – which is considered to bring good luck. Peasants in southern France also used to believe in special cats which, if treated well, would bring good fortune to their owners. Known as *matagots*, the best-known example is in the old folk-tale which we know today as *Puss-in-Boots*, but which has been told in many forms. A famous English *matagot* was the cat belonging to Dick Whittington, the poor country boy who became Lord Mayor of London. Sadly, that well-known tale is probably not literally true: the cat which brought him fortune was more likely not one which miaowed but an *achat*, a purchase or lucky trading deal, or it may have been a catboat, a one-masted vessel used in the lucrative coal trade between Newcastle-upon-Tyne and London.

In Britain black cats are usually considered lucky – but an American superstition says they bring bad luck and that if one crosses your path you should take off your hat and turn it completely around to avoid the bad luck, although it is lucky to have a grey cat pass in front of you. The Japanese think a tortoiseshell cat is lucky – and sailors used to think it could frighten storm demons away if sent to the top of the mast. White cats are lucky in America and some countries of Europe – but unlucky in Britain, where some coastal communities used to believe that their fisherfolk would return safely from sea if a black cat were kept in the house. There are still a lot of superstitions about cats. One custom, which has occasionally come to light when old buildings have been demolished or rebuilt, was the burial of a cat in the walls or foundations as a charm to bring luck, to keep rats away or perhaps as a building sacrifice.

Lucky or unlucky, the cat survived. 'Harmless and necessary' Shakespeare called it. So it has proved, and over the centuries has gained many enthusiasts. Painters and poets have celebrated its charms and its misdemeanours. In cottage and palace it found a home – but, while one cat might find a particular place in one person's affections, until quite recently, no attempt seems to have been made to breed cats selectively as dogs were bred: as guards, retrievers, herders, trackers, war dogs and fighters. It was not until the middle of the nineteenth century that people began to select cats to maintain or develop particular characteristics and then they were those of appearance rather than skill. These nineteenth-century cat enthusiasts naturally began to compare their animals and to judge them against each other.

The first real cat show seems to have been held at the Crystal Palace in London in 1871, when 170 cats were exhibited. To have set up such an event there must have already been close contact between the cat enthusiasts, but it was not until 1887 that the first major cat club was established. This was the National Cat Club, which began a stud book and register of cats. Later it developed into the single British national organization, the Governing Council of the Cat Fancy, set up in 1919, under which are gathered all the clubs and associations devoted to the various breeds, or for different localities. All standards, the strict criteria to which a particular breed must conform, are controlled by the Governing Council, who also make the decision as to whether or not a new breed shall be recognized.

The first American cat show was held in 1884 as part of a wider pet and livestock show. One arranged by an Englishman and held in New York's Madison Square Garden in 1895 was the first devoted solely to cats. A Maine Coon [see page 61] was judged the best cat in the show. The first cat club in the USA, the Beresford Cat Club of Chicago, published its first Stud Book in 1889. Other clubs followed and unity was not preserved in the United States so that now there are a number of different associations each of which establishes its own breed standards and its own rules for the conduct of shows.

The standards which the associations all over the world decide upon are not unchangeable. Refinement of a breed may make an association decide to disallow a feature which had previously been acceptable – faint tabby markings perhaps, which persist in some solid colour breeds – and they may decide to recognize a newly developed breed from time to time. Tastes change and democratic bodies change their rules to match.

Show rules too will vary according to the show. Some will be open only to members of a club, others

Above: Tabby coats come in two quite different patterns. This is the mackerel or tiger stripe which is closer to the usual wildcat patterns.

Left: The other tabby pattern is the standard or blotched, now the most common in Europe and America, with a large whorl-shape on the flanks, but the white markings are not permitted in the recognized tabby breed.

Opposite, top: A handsome Tortoiseshell and White Shorthair. The proportion of white to other colours is strictly defined in the breed description. The symmetrical marking of the face would probably find favour with the judges. Tortoiseshell and Tortoiseshell and White cats are nearly always female, and have to be mated with self-coloured black, cream or red cats to produce tortoiseshell kittens.

anyone can enter. Some are for pedigree cats only, others have classes for household pets. Information about a particular show may be obtained from the organisers or a cat club. Going to shows offers opportunities to find out about showing, breeding and all kinds of feline affairs, for cat fanciers are often cat fanatics and only too glad to talk about their subject.

Cat breeders of the recognized breeds (or of new strains which they hope will be recognized) register their cats and their cats' offspring with the organization to which they belong and are issued with certificates noting the cat's ancestry, its official name and other information. This record of a cat's family tree is its pedigree. All cats have a pedigree – but no one bothers to keep a record of cats that do not belong to the recognized breeds so that, in effect, a pedigree cat has come to mean a cat which

A Blue-cream Longhair has softly intermingling colours in Britain, but in America this Persian type must have them clearly separated. Blue-cream is a dilute form of tortoiseshell, so these females have to breed with blue or cream self-coloured cats to produce blue-cream kittens.

belongs to, and matches the requirements for, a distinct variety. They are usually more expensive to buy than non-pedigree cats – mongrels or moggies as they are often called – but they do not necessarily make better pets. The differences will be that if you mate pedigree animals you can predict what their offspring will be.

Long before the first cat clubs were formed and the first cat shows held there were people who were concerned about the way in which animals were treated. Back in 1822 the British House of Commons passed an Act giving protection to domestic animals. To ensure that it was put into force a clergyman, the Reverend Arthur Broome, decided to employ inspectors to make it effective and called a meeting of people who supported him. From that meeting the Society for the Prevention of Cruelty to Animals was formed in 1824. When Queen Victoria came to the throne she gave it her patronage and since then the Royal Society for the Prevention of Cruelty to Animals (RSPCA) has grown from one inspector to a large organization looking after the interests of animals of all kinds. Similar organizations have developed in other countries, such as the American SPCA, formed in 1866. Other organizations such as the People's Dispensary for Sick Animals (PDSA), established in 1917, and the Blue Cross, have come into existence to provide veterinary treatment for animals whose owners cannot afford private veterinary fees. These and similar bodies, like the Cats' Protection League in Britain, now help to protect and look after cats in many countries of the world. More recently they have been joined in Britain by the Feline Advisory Bureau, which not only gives advice to cat owners but also sponsors research into cat disorders, and in America by the American Feline Society. Such organizations all rely upon public subscription. They are always ready to help – but cannot do so without money.

Choosing a Cat

'All cats are grey in the dark' says the old proverb – and all cats do share basic feline characteristics but they are not all the same, cats can be as different as people. Choosing a cat is not something to do hastily. You should give a great deal of consideration to deciding what kind of cat you would like and should think hard about why you want a cat at all and whether you are able to provide the things that it will need.

Many people are tempted by the charm of a cuddly kitten into offering it a home – and far too many people decide a few months later on that the adult cat is just a nuisance and want to get rid of it. Animal welfare organizations have the unhappy task of ending the lives of thousands of perfectly healthy cats (and dogs) because of human thoughtlessness. It is very important to weigh up the demands a cat will make before taking on the responsibility for another life.

'But cats look after themselves' some people think. It is true, they can, but in practice their owner will be responsible for finding food, providing medical care when necessary, providing cat litter if they do not roam free, and will either have to be around to do these things, or be able to arrange for someone else to do them if the owner is away from home. At holiday times the cat may have to be put into boarding accommodation at a cattery. A can of cat food is not likely to break anybody's budget, but multiply that cost by the days in the year, and take into account vet's bills and boarding fees, and it will come to quite a tidy sum.

Its speckled tummy and sharp claws are a reminder that this is not just a cuddly kitten but as vigorous and resourceful as its big cat relatives.

Left: Dogs and cats can be the best of friends but this kitten is doing its best to frighten its new acquaintance. The raised fur and arched back are an instinctive reaction when danger threatens.

Below: A well-cared-for cat makes a delightful pet and will amply reward the attention it is given.

Who could resist these mongrel kittens? But no one should take home a cat without understanding the responsibilities involved.

'Why a cat?' is another question that you might try to answer, or indeed, 'Why a pet at all?' Animals offer companionship, something to care for as well as being a constant source of interest. There is evidence that they are of actual therapeutic value. A pet appears to help people, especially the convalescent and the elderly, to recover from disability or surgery and to have more purpose in life. A pet can be a source of much needed physical contact and an object both giving and demanding love and dependence. No one should feel awkward at the idea of wanting a cat for company, or for any other reason, but these are all factors to take into account when choosing a pet. Would you prefer a dog? If the answer is 'Yes', but you do not think that you could keep one in your home, then look at the possibility of small dogs. If you feel a dog would be too much trouble then perhaps a cat would be too much trouble too! However, if you keep irregular hours and therefore could not walk a dog at regular times a cat will be more independent of your coming and going – though not necessarily more tolerant.

It is often suggested that there are cat people and dog people and that they are mutually exclusive groups. However, people who like animals often like both cats *and* dogs and the tolerance with which the two species can live together belies their traditional antagonism. Dogs are as likely to chase a cat as a rabbit, if encouraged to do so, and a cat will defend itself and its territory if forced to do so, but cats and dogs that know each other will often be devoted friends.

If you do decide to have a cat, what sort should you choose? You may have seen a particular type of cat and decided that for purely aesthetic reasons you must have a cat of that breed. You may have seen an individual cat and decided that that particular animal has a special appeal for you. *You* may have been chosen by a stray cat, or be taking over a cat from someone else who is no longer able to look after it. In all these cases the decision appears to be made – but you still need to make sure that the match is as good as you think it is and to think carefully about the demands that the cat will make.

The advantage of a pedigree cat is that you can be sure what a kitten will look like when it grows up and that if bred to another cat of the same breed it will breed true. Some breeds have gained reputations for particular character traits but these have possibly been influenced as much by the way in which a line has been raised and the attitudes of the type of people who choose that type of cat as by any hereditary factors. Orientals do tend to be more demanding cats, requiring company, human or animal, and wanting to be involved in their owner's activities (or to involve their owners in their games). If you have never heard a Siamese make sure that you do before acquiring one. Some people find the Siamese voice harsh and disturbing, and they are certainly the most talkative of cats. The call of a Siamese female on heat is as raucous as the cry of a peacock – so be warned! Longhairs tend to be less energetic than shorthairs and more placid in temperament – but there are some exceedingly lively, even neurotic, longhairs too. Whether pedigree or moggie cat, if you know its mother – and especially if you know the father too – the parental personalities will give you much more guide to likely character than coat or colour.

A pedigree animal will certainly cost you more than a mongrel cat. You can get a list of breeders from the cat associations and arrange to visit them to choose a cat. Cat breeders do not usually breed cats to make a lot of money – few do – but because they love them. They may ask you as many questions as

Right: Siamese cats, like this Blue Point and Seal Point, like human company and can be very demanding.

Longhaired cats, like these two Blues and a Chinchilla, need much more grooming than shorthaired cats.

you ask them, for they want to make sure that you will provide a good home. A breeder who gives you a thorough grilling will probably be one of the most careful about the way his or her cattery is run. It is not difficult to get an idea of whether the cats are being bred under good conditions, just look around on your visit. Do not expect that you will be able to take a cat away with you. Even if there are kittens of the right age they may have been promised long before to someone else. If you plan ahead you can put your name down for a kitten from a future litter of a cat you like. If you are looking only for a household pet and do not want to breed or show, then tell the breeder. He or she may have lovely kittens which do not perfectly conform with the show standards that are less expensive: you may even find them *more* attractive.

Instead of going directly to a breeder you may get your cat from a pet store, but for a pedigree cat it is likely that the best kittens will

Above: Mongrels can make just as delightful pets as any pedigree cats.

Opposite: If you prefer a pedigree, then a longhaired breed, such as this Tortie and White, needs a great deal of attention to keep its coat free from matts and tangles.

have been sold directly from the cattery. Again you will want to be sure that the animals are kept under good conditions. Some stores do not keep animals for sale in the shop (except for fish, reptiles and very small mammals such as mice and gerbils which live in tanks or cages) but act as agents for a cattery. They will bring kittens in from breeders especially for you so that the animals have the advantage of being kept in good cattery conditions rather than a pen in the store.

You may also get a cat from a refuge run by one of the animal protection societies. Most cats there will be mongrels and you will also find many older cats. When thinking of getting a cat most people automatically think of a kitten, but there are always adult cats that need homes and for some people they may be a better choice. An older cat will be quieter and more settled in its behaviour. Young kittens can be boisterous, even accidentally destructive until they have been trained, and need both constant reassurance after being separated from their mothers and constant watching to make sure that they get up to no harm to themselves or to your belongings. An older, less mobile person may find a small kitten, always under their feet, a problem. Someone who has to be away from home all day, leaving the cat alone, might find it easier to accommodate an older cat which has already been trained.

If you take over an older cat from someone you know you have prior knowledge of its general character and temperament and its health record. But do not be pressured into giving a cat a home. If you are not fully prepared to accept the responsibility and expense of caring for it you should refuse.

Sometimes the choice will not be up to you. A stray or a deserted cat may come asking to be adopted or just move in with you. Should this happen you should first try to trace the original owner – he or she may be desperately worried about the cat. If it wears a collar with an identification disc you will have an address or telephone number to contact. Some owners have an identification number tattooed on the inner leg of cats and dogs since this cannot be removed if an animal is stolen. Check no loss has been reported to the police. Put a notice on a tree or post near where you found the cat, in local shops and vets' waiting rooms and see if your local newspapers will publish an announcement. When you are quite sure that the owner is untraceable, or if the owner does not want his or her animal back, you can consider the visitor your own pet.

However, assuming you are choosing a cat, the decision about exact breed and colour will be one largely of appearance, but whether mongrel or pedigree you should bear in mind that a longhaired cat will need more attention to its coat. Daily grooming is required, ignoring it may lead to even more time-consuming sessions to remove matts and tangles from the fur. Foreign shorthairs need much less grooming but will not like being left alone for long periods in an apartment: if you are going to keep an oriental as a housebound cat, and there are no other animals to keep it company, think of having a pair, not a bad idea with any cats.

Should you have a male or a female? Unless you intend to raise kittens it does not make a great deal of difference, for pet tom-cats

should be neutered. There are far too many unwanted kittens born and you should ensure that your cat does not add to them. An unneutered tom will spray urine to mark his teritory, leaving an all-pervading odour around your home. His sex drive will send him on the prowl for mates and he will get into scraps with other toms. If you want to have a breeding tom take advice from experienced breeders on the best ways to keep him. It would be anti-social to keep an unneutered mongrel. Females can also have their sex organs removed (spaying). It is a commonplace operation for vets, although more complicated than castration. If it is not done you will either have to keep your cat locked up whenever it is in season (something not always easy to distinguish), or to be prepared to find yourself with a litter of kittens twice a year. Some people like to let a female have at least one litter before the operation is carried out, for spaying can be done at any time, although it is easier in a younger cat. Castration is best done shortly before the cat reaches maturity, at about six months old. If left too late the spraying and roaming pattern may already have been established.

When choosing an individual kitten look for the strongest and fittest, suppress your sympathy for the runt of the litter or the sad and sickly bundle in the corner of the pet shop pen. This is advice that many people ignore, they are drawn by those in obvious need, but often they have an uphill struggle to rear the cat to health and there can be tragedy and heartbreak if they fail to do so, or a lifetime of veterinary visits and bills. You may be lucky, but look at the situation unemotionally: so many healthy kittens are humanely destroyed each year that it is only realistic to give the fit animals the first chance of survival, rather than those who may not make it.

If you cannot make up your mind between two kittens why not have both? These Seal Point Siamese kittens make perfect playmates for each other.

Look at the whole litter, for any sign of disease in one will raise doubts about all of them. Look at the eyes: they should be bright and clear with no signs of discharge and the nictitating membrane should not be raised. Look at the nostrils: they should be clean and dry. Look at the ears: they should be clean and smell sweet, with a slightly moist look inside and no sign of discharge; dark specks of dirt or a brownish fluid are indications of the presence of ear parasites. The kitten's body should be firm: if the stomach seems distended this may indicate that there are internal worms. Check the fur: it should be clean and without any black specks which might be flea excreta, there should not be any signs of scabs or scratching which could indicate a skin disorder; check below the tail for any yellow staining or other sign of diarrhoea, which is one of the symptoms of enteritis and of other troubles.

Unless you have disturbed them at a normal sleeping time all the kittens should be lively and interested. Watch their movements. Very young kittens may be a little unstable on their feet but by the time you would be permitted to see them they should be well-balanced and moving confidently.

Often one kitten in a litter will tend to dominate the others. It will probably be the biggest – because it has pushed the others out of the way to get more than its share of its mother's milk and food. This will probably be a very healthy cat but it may also develop into a bossy one, difficult to discipline. Unless you are prepared for that, choose one not so over-confident, but equally avoid the over-shy and timid, which may have personality problems in the other direction. Nevertheless, you will probably lose your heart to one kitten that comes over and chooses you and will pay no attention to this advice whatever!

In otherwise healthy cats fleas, ear mites and even internal worms can be easily treated; if left un-

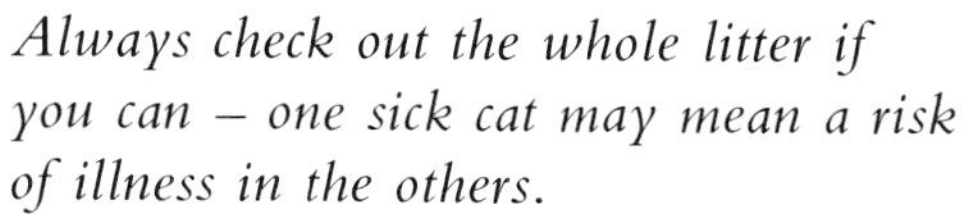

Always check out the whole litter if you can – one sick cat may mean a risk of illness in the others.

treated and severe infestations are allowed to develop, they will undermine a kitten's health. If a breeder or pet dealer attempts to hide or ignore defects proceed with care. Any reputable person will agree to you purchasing a cat subject to a veterinary inspection and if you have any doubt about an animal's good health you should insist that the kitten can be returned if there are veterinary problems found at that inspection. All young kittens should be inoculated against the major cat disease Feline infectious enteritis, or Panleukopenia. This is an highly infectious viral disease which attacks the blood-forming system, leading to a deficiency of white corpuscles. Its progress is rapid and usually fatal. No treatment is known but cats which have been inoculated against it, even if not totally immune, may have sufficient resistance to fight the disease and, with careful nursing, can survive. It is essential that all kittens be inoculated and if the breeder does not give you a certificate signed by a veterinary surgeon showing that this has been done it should be undertaken as soon as possible and booster doses given at intervals throughout the cat's life. Even if a kitten has had its shots it is a good idea to have a general check-up with a vet and to get advice as to when your practitioner prefers to neuter.

A kitten should stay with its mother until it is at least seven, and usually eight weeks old. Some breeders will insist on keeping them together for longer. Even though a kitten may seem quite independent and to have become attached to you do not think of taking it away before this age. It will still be quite young enough to respond to your personal training and there will be plenty of grow-

Look out for lively kittens with bright eyes and clean coats like these three.

NAME OF CAT SOLITAIRE MAOLI & SOLITAIRE MOANIANI
BREED No. 29 GCCF No. SR/NS 40294 (M) 40295 (F)
SEX Male & female
COLOUR and MARKINGS Havana Brown
DATE OF BIRTH 1-4-77
OWNER

pedigree

SOLITAIRE CATTERY
HUNTING GROVE
LOWFIELD HEATH · CRAWLEY · SUSSEX

Seal, Chocolate, Blue, Lilac, Red, Tortie, Tabby Pointed and all dilute-colour Siamese.
Burmese, and exotic Foreign Shorthairs.

BREEDER: MRS. ANGELA SAYER
Telephone: Crawley 23470

PARENTS	GRANDPARENTS	GREAT GRANDPARENTS	GT. GT. GRANDPARENTS
SIRE SOLITAIRE MIDNIGHT COWBOY Breed No: 26 (Foreign Black) GCCF No: 259470	SISLINKI TAMIL 24	CH SISLINKI TOPAL 24	CH STARSHINE BANDIDO 24
			SUPRA FLIRT 24
		KARIBUR JARNA 24b	ROUNDWAY OURISIA 24b
			CH REOKY SHIM-WAH 24b
	SOLITAIRE KAIULANI 29	CH DANDYCAT ZULU WARRIOR 29	CH WINCEBY IMPERIAL 24c
			CH SCINTILLA COPPER BEECH 29
		CH DANDYCAT HULA DANCER 29	CH TIJHA ARES 24c
			CH SCINTILLA COPPER BEECH 29
DAM SOLITAIRE ANIANI Breed No: 29 GCCF No: SR/NS 26652	CH ZAMAAZI ZOLITAIRE 29	CH DANDYCAT BROWN BEAR 29	CH TIJHA ARES 24c
			CH SCINTILLA COPPER BEECH 29
		DINWOODIE ORANSHEE 24b	CH SUNJADE CHOCOLATE DOMINO 24b
			MYCALDOR LUCY 24c
	SOLITAIRE AALA 29	CH SOLITAIRE MANEKI NEKO 29	CH FLORENTINE M'BELE 29
			SOLITAIRE GARNET 24b
		CH SOLITAIRE TIARE TAHITI 29	HAZELWOOD APOLLO 24b
			CH DANDYCAT HULA DANCER 29

I certify this Pedigree to be correct to the best of my knowledge. Signed Angela Sayer Date 17.7.77.

ing up to share with it as it goes through kittenhood, but it has to learn some of the basic skills of life, that only its mother can teach it, to become capable of independence.

Ask the breeder for his or her advice on matters of diet and other care for, even though you may later establish a different regimen, it is best to aid the transfer to a new home by keeping as many things the same as possible. If you are taking on an older cat this will be even more important, for it will have established habits and these must be taken into account when teaching it a new set of rules.

If a cat is a pedigree animal make sure that you have its pedigree documentation and registration certificate and that change of ownership is recorded, or arrange for these matters to be dealt with promptly. If you intend to breed yourself it is essential to have these things in order. The breeder will also be able to tell you the address of the registrar, the procedures for making registrations, and so on.

Most breeders become very attached to their animals, and no matter how many cats they have reared they will often welcome news of cats that they have bred. You should also let them know if any serious problems develop which could be of an hereditary nature for, if a line should prove to be producing unfit animals, they will not want to continue breeding from it.

Top: A typical pedigree form.

Above: When a kitten leaves its mother it should be fully weaned and eating a variety of solid foods.

Shorthaired Cats

All the early domestic cats of North Africa and Europe were shorthaired cats. Some of the coat colours and patterns we know today were established long ago but the exact requirements for the pedigree breeds are of comparatively recent date. A cat may quite accurately be described as a shorthaired tabby or a black cat with short hair without necessarily being of a type that would qualify as belonging to that breed.

Over the years cat breeders vary as to the way in which they interpret the 'standards' laid down for each type according to the prevailing taste among them, and after a strain has bred true for several generations the world's various cat bodies may agree to accept a new colour, pattern or variety – nevertheless, the appearance required for every type is very strictly set down.

European and North American requirements are usually very close but there are two distinct types of shorthaired domestic cat which reflect separate development on the two sides of the Atlantic.

The British Blue, with its fine plush coat, is the epitome of British Shorthairs.

British Shorthairs

The British (and European) shorthair is sturdy and well-built with powerful muscles on a strong-boned skeleton. It is well-fleshed but not fat. The body is of medium length and correspondingly rather deep from back to stomach. The legs are short with rounded paws and the tail shortish, thick at the base and tapering only slightly to a rounded tip. The round, apple-shaped head is set on a short thick neck. The cheeks are full, the nose short and broad, the skull rounded and the ears small, well apart and with rounded tips. The eyes are large and round.

Fur is short and dense, the ideal is a plushy texture, and coats are recognized in a number of colours and patterns. The **British Blue** is generally considered to be the cat that matches up best to the required conformation and coat. A medium to light blue-grey fur is

Right: A Chartreaux, a French breed, almost identical to the British Blue, though it may have green eyes.

Below: British Shorthairs: Cream and Black.

now preferred to the dark slate colour which used to mark the breed. Like all British Shorthairs (unless otherwise specified) it has copper or orange eyes. Nose and paw leather match the coat. British Blues are usually placid and gentle cats of great intelligence.

The French have a breed called the **Chartreux** which the British Cat Fancy considers synonymous with the British Blue, though in France it can have green eyes and a coat of any shade of blue. Its name comes from a tradition that the breed was brought back from southern Africa by Carthusian monks. In America also it is sometimes recognized as a separate breed and expected to be rounder of face and have bigger ears than the British cat.

Other British shorthaired self-coloured cats are **Black,** with matching leather; **Cream,** with red leather; and **White,** with red leather and eyes of either orange or blue or with one of each colour. Pure white cats with blue eyes are nearly always deaf but if a kitten has the smallest patch of dark fur, which it may well lose as it gets older, it is spared this genetically-linked defect.

Tabby-patterned British Shorthairs can be Red, Brown or Silver. Markings may be either the tiger-striped mackerel pattern or the blotched standard pattern. The Silver has green or hazel eyes, black paw pads and preferably a brick-red nose, although a black nose is permitted. There are also **Spotted Shorthairs** (once known as Spotted Tabbies) in the same colours as the Tabby. Ideally their spots should be round and, although variation is permitted, they must never look like broken stripes.

Left: A Silver Tabby British Shorthair with well-defined standard, or blotched, markings.

Below: Orange-eyed White British Shorthairs. Orange eyes do not bring deafness problems.

Bi-coloured British Shorthairs have not more than half the coat white and not more than two-thirds patched with black, red, blue or cream, with no stripes or stray hairs of the wrong colour. Nose and paw pads may be pink or black or a mixture of the two.

The **Tortoiseshell British Shorthair** is evenly patched with black, cream and red. Male tortoiseshell cats are usually infertile so sires are chosen from self-coloured cats with one of these colours in their coat. Not all kittens will be tortoiseshell, and those that are often have very dark coats which become brighter in colour as they get older. Sometimes an all-black cat and an all-red cat will also produce tortoiseshell kittens.

The **Tortoiseshell and White** has similar markings predominating on the head, back, tail, paws and parts of the flanks with the

Left: A Black and White Bi-coloured British Shorthair with an elegant blaze across the nose.

Opposite, below: A Spotted British Shorthair. This hefty fellow is a tom at stud.

Below: A Tortoiseshell and White British Shorthair. Almost all these cats are female.

underparts and chin left white and, ideally, a white blaze on the face. Like the Tortoiseshell this is a female-only variety.

Other British Shorthairs are the Blue-Cream, the Smoke and the British Tipped. In the **Blue-Cream** the two colours should be softly intermingled in the coat and evenly balanced throughout, with blue nose leather and either blue or pink paw pads. **Smoke Shorthairs** may have a topcoat of either black or blue with a silver undercoat which shines through the darker colour as the animal moves. Nose and paw pads match the coat. In the **British Tipped Shorthair** both undercoat and topcoat are white but hairs on the tail, back, flanks, head and ears are tipped with colour which may be any of the self-colours described above or brown, chocolate or lilac. Nose leather and paw pads should be pink or correspond to the colour of the tipping.

American Shorthairs

The American Shorthair (or Domestic Shorthair as it is also known) originated from European shorthairs but is now a quite distinct breed. It is longer-bodied and longer-legged than the British cat,

A Blue-eyed White Shorthair.

Opposite, centre: An Odd-eyed White Shorthair. Only white cats among the pedigree breeds are allowed to have odd-coloured eyes.

Opposite, below: A Calico American Shorthair, its white coat patched with tortoiseshell.

with a much less chunky look. Its tail is heavy at the base and tapers to a blunt tip and its paws are rounded with heavy pads. The head is heart-shaped, rather than the apple-shape of the British cat and is set on a medium length neck. It also has larger ears, which are widely set but less open at the base, and its eyes have a slight hint of a slant to them. The coat of the American Shorthair consists of harsher fur than the British and comes in a much wider range of colours.

In solid colours White, Black, Blue and Red are recognized. The **White** may be blue, orange or odd-eyed (the blue-eyed being linked genetically with deafness). The **Black** has golden eyes and black or brown paw pads. In the **Blue** even coat colour is more important than shade so that a darker cat of level tone will be preferred to a light coat of uneven colour, although pale coats are liked best. **Reds** have a deep, rich-coloured coat with no shading – not even on the lips or chin – with brick red nose leather and paw pads and golden eyes. They have no parallel in Britain where tabby markings have proved so persistent in red coats that a red-self has not been recognized.

In the American Shorthair the tipped cats are recognized as quite separate varieties. The **Chinchilla American Shorthair** is a cat with a white undercoat and a topcoat tipped with black on the tail, back, flanks and head. It may also be slightly shaded on the legs but the chin, chest and underside must be pure white. The rims of the eyes, nose and lips are outlined in black and the paw pads are also black, but the nose leather is brick red. The Chinchilla's eyes may be emerald or blue-green. The **Shaded Silver American Shorthair** has slightly darker tipping than the Chinchilla and the **Shell Cameo** and **Shaded Cameo** cats are the red-tipped equivalents of the Chinchilla and Shaded Silver. They have rose-coloured nose leather and pads and bright golden eyes.

The **Smoke American Shorthair** has a jet black topcoat over a white undercoat, so that it looks solid black until the cat moves. Paw pads and nose leather are black and eyes bright gold. There are also a **Blue Smoke,** with blue topcoat, leather and pads, and a **Red Smoke** (also known as a Smoke Cameo) with red topcoat and rose leather and pads, both with golden eyes.

In tabby coats there are Silver, Brown and Red Tabby varieties, which are like those of the British cats, and also Blue, Cream and Cameo Tabbies. The **Silver Tabby** should have green or hazel eyes (unlike the usual gold or copper). The **Blue Tabby** has a ground colour of pale bluish ivory with darker blue markings, 'old rose' nose leather, rose paw pads and brilliant golden eyes. The **Cream Tabby** has a pale cream base colour with darker cream or buff markings which must stay within the genetically dilute range and not become reddish. Its nose leather and paw pads are pink and its eyes gold. The **Cameo Tabby** differs from the **Red Tabby** in having an off-white ground colour to contrast with its red markings, rose nose leather and pads. Its eyes, too, are brilliant gold.

Parti-color American Shorthairs (or Bi-colours as they are called in Britain) are white cats patched with solid colour of either black, blue, red or cream. The **Tortoiseshell** is patterned like the European type and the **Tortoiseshell and White** is also similar, although the exact amount and distribution of the white part of the cat varies slightly between the different American cat associations. Some of these associations call a cat with markings like the European Tortoiseshell the **Calico American Shorthair,** but others give this name to a cat that has an overall white coat with tri-colour patches rather than one with specific areas of white. The Calico can also be a white cat patched with black and red and lacking the cream third colour of the tortoiseshell pattern.

Red and Cream patches have also been combined with the range of tabby markings to produce another group of American Shorthair varieties known as the **Patched Tabbies.** They all have gold or hazel eyes except for the Silver Patched Tabby in which they are green or hazel.

Exotic Shorthair

This American breed was created by crossing American Shorthairs with Persian (Longhair) cats [see next chapter] to produce a type that has the physique and the dense, soft-textured hair of the Persian cat but with the fur short in length (although longer than in the Shorthair). It looks closer to the British Shorthair in type than to its American ancestor, with a cobby body on short legs, a deep chest, massive shoulders and a massive rump. The broad, round head is set on a short, thick neck. The ears are small and low set, wide apart, round-tipped and tilted forward. The short, broad nose is set between full cheeks and the eyes are large and round. The tail is short and carried straight, usually held on a lower line than the spine. Although the plushy fur is short it stands away from the body in a way distinctive of the breed. It needs much less grooming than the Persian cat. The Exotic Shorthair is recognized in all the colours of the American Shorthair and eye colour, nose leather and paw pads should follow those described for the colours of that group.

American Wirehair

This breed has a quite different kind of fur from other cats. It was developed from a chance mutation that appeared in a litter of cats on a farm in Verona, New York State. This kitten had fur like that of a Wirehair Terrier dog, although if anything even coarser, which curled tightly on the head and on the ears. Adam, the original cat, was mated to a number of American Shorthair females and all produced some kittens with their father's wire hair, showing that this must be a dominant gene. They also inherited his conformation, with rather longer legs, heavier hips and shorter heads. The breed now has gently rounded heads with rather full cheeks. The large, round eyes tilt slightly upwards in the outer corners. The ears are set well apart with slightly rounded tips. The medium-length fur is coarse and springy to the touch and especially wiry on the head, back, sides and hips and along the tail. It can be less coarse on the chin and under the body. Even the whiskers should be curly. American Wirehairs are accepted in all the American Shorthair colours and patterns with eye colour, nose colour and paw pads to match.

Bombay

The Bombay is another breed produced from the American Shorthair, this time by crossing a black cat with a Burmese [see page 73]. It retains the general type of the American Shorthair with the sleek coat of the Burmese. The close-lying fur is jet black with a sheen like patent leather. A Bombay's head is pleasantly rounded and its nose has a visible break in the profile. Its ears are of medium size, with slightly rounded tips, broad at the base, set well apart and tilting forward slightly. Its big, bright eyes are round, well spaced and range from yellow to deep copper in colour, the darker the better.

Scottish Fold

Although it is not recognized in Britain, this breed was developed there from a chance mutation which appeared in a litter of farm kittens born to a cat called Suzie in Perthshire, Scotland, in 1961: a kitten with flop-over ears. Two years later the same mother produced two more similar cats and later breeding showed that this was the result of a dominant gene. At their birth the kittens do not have the characteristic droop to the ears and in 1971 one of them won a prize in a British show, the judge taking it to be a normal prick-eared cat, but the British Cat Fancy did not recognize the breed. Close breeding in the original stock did produce some bone problems and there were suggestions that the folded ear might make the cats vulnerable to hearing problems and ear diseases, but breeders persisted with their efforts and transferred their stock to the United States where the breed has been accepted in the usual shorthair colours. Because the original kittens were bred to British Shorthairs this cat follows the conformation of the British Shorthair type with its short, soft coat. The usually small ears fold down at the top of the ear pocket, which does make them more difficult to keep clean. In kittens the fold may be only slight, but in adults it must be quite definite.

Drop ears have occasionally been reported in the past in cats but they are generally considered to occur in a species only after many centuries of domestication. They are common in dogs, which have been domesticated for far longer than cats and the breeding of which has long been under man's control.

Sphynx

This very rare and most unusual breed is recognized by only a few cat associations and not at all in Britain. It is an almost hairless cat. Such cats had appeared before, but no attempt was made to perpetuate them until one appeared in a litter born to a black and white domestic pet in Ontario, Canada, in 1966. The Sphynx has a covering of almost-invisible soft, downy hair except on the ears, muzzle, tail, feet and testicles of males, where it is denser and more noticeable. Along the spine there may also be a ridge of short wiry hair and a soft pile on the face. There are no whiskers or eyebrows. If you stroke a Sphynx it feels rather like a piece of suede. An adult's skin should be taut and wrinkle-free, except on the head where wrinkles are permitted, but kittens often have loose and puckered skin. They have a high body temperature and sweat easily but they like a warm environment and avoid lying down on cold surfaces. Breeders say that, although people-oriented and not very keen on other types of cat, they do not like being cuddled. Although they came from an American domestic cat, and were bred with American cats to develop the line, they changed type as well as hair length and have a longish head with a clear stop at the bridge of the nose, a long slender neck, a medium long body and a longish tapering tail. A rather barrel chest tends to make the legs look bowed but the feet are oval and dainty. Sphynx cats can be any of the accepted American Shorthair colours.

Rex cats

Rex cats are another breed – or in Europe two separate breeds – with extraordinary fur. Most cats have a coat made up of long, straight, thick hairs which taper evenly (guard hairs), curving hairs which thicken and then taper suddenly (awn hairs) and crimped hairs, somewhere between the two, plus others which are evenly thin, crimped hairs (down hairs) which are much more numerous than the others. In the Rex coat there are only down hairs (or in the case of the German Rex a few awned down hairs too) which are only about half as long as those of the normal cat. This makes the fur much less dense, giving a short, plushy coat with a wavy effect which is especially noticeable as ripples down the back. Whiskers

Opposite, top: The Scottish Fold, the only breed with droopy ears, was discovered in Britain but not accepted there as an official breed.
Below: The curly coat of the Cornish Rex is made up of a different balance of hair types from other cats.

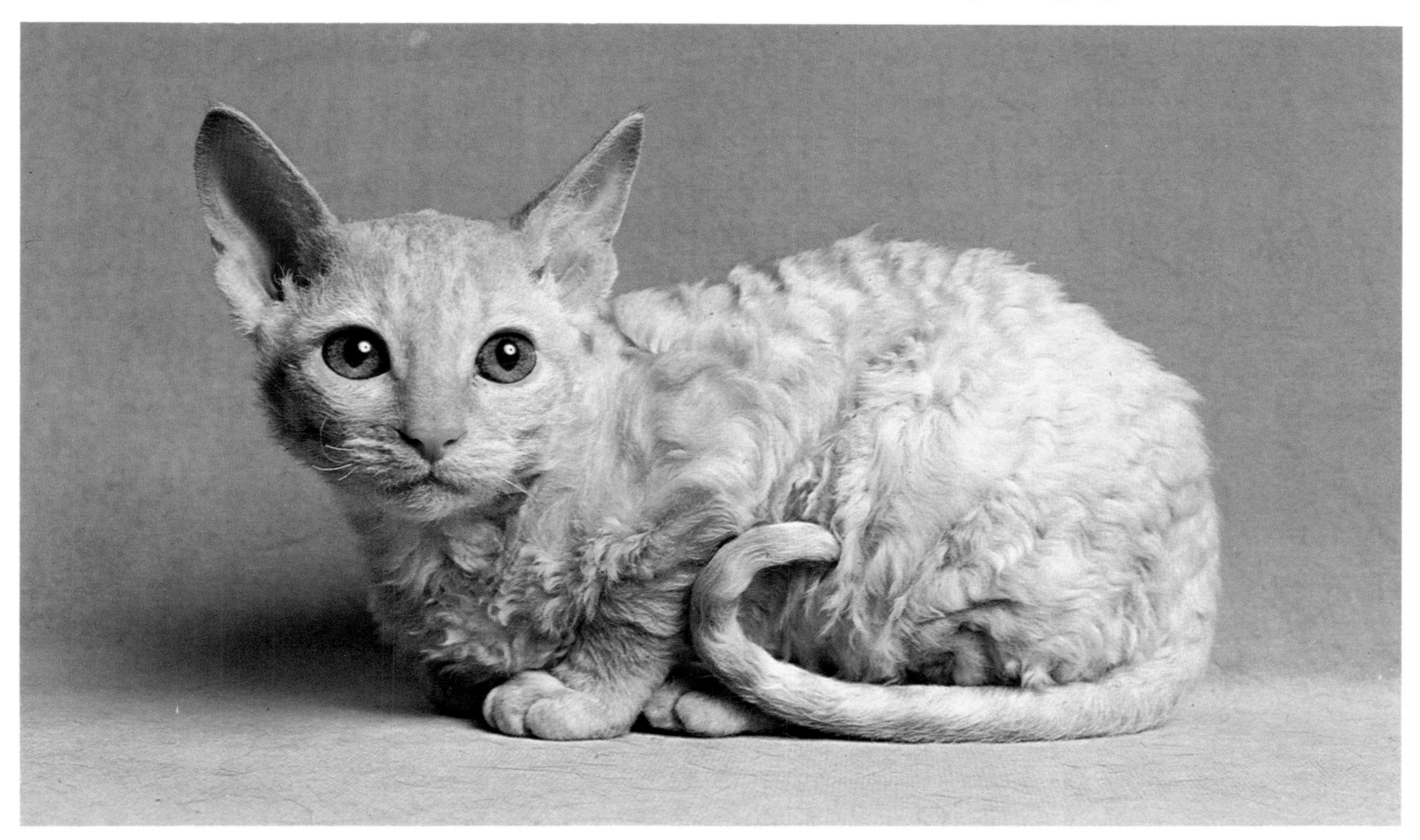

and eyebrows are both crinkly hair.

The first known cat with this kind of coat was already several years old when discovered among the cats living in the grounds of a hospital in East Berlin in 1951. It was given the name *Lämmchen*, because of its lamb-like fur. This cat produced kittens with a similar curly coat and several of its progeny were taken to the United States, where they became the foundation of the North American Rex. Similar mutations were also discovered in Ohio in 1953 and in Oregon in 1958.

In Britain a kitten with Rex fur was born in an otherwise normal litter at Bodmin, Cornwall, in 1950. Its mother was a tortoiseshell and white shorthaired cat, its father was unknown. This cat was several times mated back to its mother and about half of the resulting kittens had curly coats. From them the Cornish Rex has been developed. American breeders have claimed successful matings between the German and Cornish types.

Ten years later another curly-coated kitten appeared in the neighbouring English county of Devon. This proved to be incompatible with the Cornish type (cross-matings produced only normal coats) and a new mutation, the origin of what, in Britain, is regarded as a separate breed: the Devon Rex.

Although descending from ordinary domestic cats all the Rex types look more foreign in type than British or American Shorthairs and are often grouped with the Foreign Shorthairs for show purposes. The **Cornish** has long, straight legs with small oval paws and a long tapering tail. Its head is slightly wedge-shaped and its large ears are high-set with rounded tips. Its coat can be any colour but any white markings must be symmetrical, except in tortoiseshell and white. The oval eyes should be of an appropriate colour for the coat.

The **Devon Rex** has a broader chest and shorter back than the Cornish Rex and its head is distinctively different, with full cheeks and a distinct break on the nose. The muzzle is short and the whisker pads are very noticeable. The ears are large and low set, tapering to rounded tops, and the eyes are slightly oval. All colours except bi-colours are acceptable and white markings are considered a fault, except in the tortoiseshell and white. The eye colour should be chartreuse, green or yellow according to the coat. Si-Rex are considered to be part of the same breed but show the Siamese point pattern and have blue eyes.

Manx

The Manx is a cat without a tail – but cats without tails have occured at many times and in many places and the Manx has many other characteristic features which distinguish it from the British Shorthair, the type it most resembles. Its head is somewhat larger, although without approaching the Persian type, with a longish nose, though the cheeks are quite full, giving it a roundness. In America some breeders prefer a definite dip in the

Right: A full Manx should have a rump as rounded as an apple. This is a fine example of their conformation but it does not match any of the British standard colours.

Si-Rex are Siamese cats with a Rex coat.

nose. The ears are set well apart and are wide at the base, tapering to a point at the tip. The back is short, and, because the hind legs are longer than the front ones, the rump is carried higher than the rest of the back. These long hind legs give the Manx a powerful spring and make it a faster running cat than most. The rump should be well-rounded, with no vestige of a tail, indeed it should be possible to feel a hollow at the end of the backbone. Some Manx have a small tuft of fur where a tail would be; this is acceptable provided that it contains no cartilage or bone. The high rump and deep flank help to give the cat a bobbing gait, somewhat like that of a rabbit.

The Manx fur is a special double coat, soft and open – another rabbit-like feature – with a short, thick undercoat. It can be of any colour and pattern but the eye colour must match the coat according to the standards laid down for British Shorthairs.

The Manx takes its name from the Isle of Man, between Britain and Ireland, and this tailless strain does seem to have developed there. Some people claim that it sprang from cats which swam ashore from a ship in Philip II's Spanish Armada, which was wrecked as it sailed round England. On the island the Manx is often known as a Rumpy. Even when bred Rumpy to Rumpy, Manx litters may include cats with partial or complete tails and a Stumpy (short-tailed) and Tailed Manx are now recognized. Some American associations recognize as many as five different forms of Manx: Rumpy, Riser (with a small number of caudal vertebrae which can be felt or seen), Stubby (with a distinct and movable short tail), Longy (still less than full-length tail) and Tailed.

Unfortunately the genetic coding that causes taillessness can be linked with physical and health problems. The lack of vertebrae may extend further than the tail and a malfunction of the sphincter muscles is also associated with the malformation. For this reason Manx are rarely bred Rumpy to Rumpy and are sometimes bred to other tailed cats, although breeding within the Manx strain is preferable to retain its particular conformation.

Longhaired Cats

None of the wild species of the cat family has long hair and in feral cat populations it takes only a generation or two for long hair to revert to short hair, so short hair is clearly the basic type. There is no record of longhaired cats in Europe until the sixteenth century when travellers introduced them as curiosities from Turkey and Persia. The Turkish type became known as the Angora (from a form of the name of the city, Ankara, which is now the Turkish capital) and the name was probably used for most kinds of longhaired cat until the nineteenth century when the cat enthusiasts who were taking breeding seriously began to favour the heavier Persian type. The Angora nearly disappeared but a breeding programme begun at the Ankara zoo preserved the variety and with cats taken to America from the zoo in the 1960s the breed was re-established in the United States and then elsewhere, although it has not yet reached sufficient numbers to be registered in Britain.

Angora

The Angora has a longish body and its legs are long with small, round paws, the back legs being longer than the front ones so that the back rises to the rear when the cat is standing. The tail is long and tapering and often carried curved forward over the back when the cat is on the move. The wedge-shaped head is small and neat with large, upright ears and big, almond-shaped eyes, which slope slightly upwards. The coat is of medium length and rather wavy, especially on the stomach. There are tufts of fur at the ear tips and between the toes and plenty of hair in the ears.

The cats at the Ankara zoo are all white and that was the only colour recognized at first in the United States, with pink nose, lips and paw pads and blue or amber eyes (or one of each) – blue eyes and white coat together carrying the usual risk of deafness. Now American associations recognize a variety of colours: Black, Blue, Black Smoke, Blue Smoke, Calico, Particolor and Tabbies of Silver, Brown, Red or Blue. Leather and paw pads should be those usual for

Above: One of the new varieties of Angora which have appeared in recent years.

Opposite: An orange-eyed White Longhair (Persian) with a fine ruff and bushy tail.

the coat in Longhair (Persian) cats [see below] and all except the green- or hazel-eyed Silver Tabby should have amber eyes.

Longhairs (Persians)

The Persian cat is now officially known as the Longhair by the British Cat Fancy but in America it is still called the Persian by most cat associations. The standards generally apply to both sides of the Atlantic. The type has changed since it first became so popular a century ago and is probably now more extreme, with even longer and more luxuriant fur. It now should have a cobby body (massive and low-lying) set on short thick legs. The tail is short, though in proportion to the body, and does not taper. The feet are large and round, with the toes set close together. The back is level, the chest

Opposite, top: A Red Longhair (Persian). Red-self cats with no tabby markings are very difficult to breed.

Opposite, below: The Lilac Longhair has only been recognized as a breed in recent years.

Left: A blue-eyed White Longhair (Persian).

Below: The Blue Longhair (Persian) is a smoky grey-blue colour.

deep and a short, sturdy neck carries a massive head which is round and broad with full cheeks and a short nose. American standards ask for a definite break or 'stop' where the nose meets the forehead. The ears are small, set low on the head and far apart. They tilt forward slightly, are not very wide at the base and have rounded tips. The eyes are round and large and, except for the White, Silver Tabbies and the Chinchilla, should be copper-coloured.

The coat is long and thick and, especially when well brushed, will stand away from the body so that it is not easy to distinguish the body shape. The fine silky hair is extremely long around the neck, forming a ruff which extends down over the chest, and on the tail forming a bush of fur. There are also long tufts on the ears and between the toes.

The breed is recognized in many colour varieties. The British Cat Fancy and the American associations recognize self-coloured **White** (with orange, blue or odd eyes), which has pink nose leather and paw pads; **Black,** with black nose leather and paw pads; **Blue,** with blue leather and pads; **Red,** with brick-red leather and pads;

and **Cream,** with pink leather and pads. The Blue-eyed White is likely to have hearing problems [see page 42]. Originally only this eye-colour was known but Whites probably had a stronger element of Angora ancestry than other colours and were bred to Blue Longhairs to correct this, thereby introducing the orange eye colour. Blacks must not have a single white hair in the coat – pure jet black is required. Especially in moult, or when a cat has been basking for a long time in summer sunshine, a rustiness may appear in the fur, but this should revert to a good black later. In the Blue American standards give preference to lighter shades, although evenness of colour is more important; in Britain it may be any shade, provided it is free of white or other colour hairs. Reds tend to retain some tabby markings, but this is less noticeable in a longhair than in short-haired cats, so the colour is recognized in longhairs on both sides of the Atlantic. Kittens which have very strong markings sometimes turn out to be excellent Reds by the time they have got their full adult coat – which may take up to two years to achieve. Whiskers should also be red, as should lips and chin, which spoil many cats by being cream or even white. The Cream is a dilute form of Red.

On both sides of the Atlantic Silver, Brown and Red Tabby Longhairs are recognized. In

America Cream, Blue and Cameo Tabby Persians can all be registered and shown. The British Fancy has also provisionally recognized Chocolate and Lilac Longhairs. Markings follow the same patterns as in shorthaired cats, although in longhairs the pattern is not quite so distinct. The **Silver Tabby** has red nose leather and black paw pads with bright green or hazel eyes, and with its black markings against a silver ground, can be a very beautiful cat. The **Brown Tabby** is tawny brown with black markings, red nose leather and pink paw pads. The ground colour of the **Cream Tabby** coat should be pale cream, including the lips and chin, marked with a darker cream or buff, with pink nose leather and paw pads. The deep blue markings of the **Blue Tabby** are offset against a bluish ivory and the whole coat has a warm fawn overtone. Nose leather and paw pads in this variety are old rose and rose. The **Cameo** has an off-white ground colour with red markings and nose leather and paw pads of rose. All except the Silver Tabby have bright copper eyes, or gold is acceptable in the American breeds.

There is another red American breed which may be either self-colour or tabby-patterned. Known as the **Peke-faced Persian**, it has a particularly squashed-in face – like that of a Pekinese dog – which carries the Persian look to its extreme. Its large round eyes are somewhat prominent and heavy wrinkles run down from the eyes on either side of its upturned nose. As in pugs and Pekinese dogs, a cat with this kind of face can have breathing difficulties and sometimes the fold of skin beneath the

Below: A Brown Tabby Longhair (Persian).

Bottom: A Silver Tabby Longhair (Persian). Tabby markings are not so distinct in longhaired cats.

A Blue-cream Longhair. The American Blue-cream Persian does not have the colours intermingled.

eyes can engender blocked tear ducts, so breeders have to be very careful to eliminate such problems. In Britain the breed is not recognized and its development has been discouraged because of the risk of producing cats which may suffer from those difficulties or from actual deformities.

In Britain **Bi-coloured Longhairs** may be of any solid colour and white, but in North America, where the variety is known as the **Parti-colored Persian**, it must be white with either black, blue, red or cream. The patching should be very clearly defined and the face should be patched, a white blaze between the nose and forehead and an inverted white V over the face being particularly favoured. Nose and paw pads should match the coat colours.

In America the **Blue-cream Persian** should also be distinctly patched, and a cream blaze on the forehead is desirable, but in Britain the **Blue-cream Longhair** should have intermingled colours so that the coat looks rather like shot silk.

Tortoiseshell Longhairs should have their red, cream and black patching evenly distributed – black should never be dominant – but separation will not be quite so clear as in the shorthairs. The American **Tortoiseshell and White Persian** is patterned like the Shorthair, with white feet, legs and underparts, the white extending halfway up the body with white splashes on the nose and halfway around the neck, but the British **Tortoiseshell and White Longhair** standard differs from the Shorthair in requiring only a good balance

Right: Tortoiseshell Longhairs (Persians).

Below: A Tortoiseshell and White Longhair (Persian).

between the colours, the patching being interspersed with white, rather than laying down where the patterning or white should be.

In some American associations the **Calico Persian** follows the requirements of the British Tortoiseshell and White but others specify a white ground patched with red and black, or patched with red, cream and black, with the belly mainly white and white areas on chest, legs, paws and face. Usually there is more white in a Calico coat than in that of the Tortoiseshell and White. The **Dilute Calico Persian** is like the Calico, except that the patching is of blue and cream on white, the white predominating on the underparts.

The **Chinchilla Persian** has a pure white undercoat with a top-coat of long, silky fur tipped with black upon the back, flanks, tail, head and ears. In North America, where it is sometimes known as the Silver Persian, it is like the other Persians in everything except coat and eye colour, but in Britain it is usually a smaller and more dainty-looking cat. Its eyes are emerald or blue green, not the usual copper, and both they and the brick-red nose are outlined by black skin. Paw pads are also black. Chinchilla kittens are frequently born with dark fur, and often with tabby markings, especially on the tail, but these disappear as they get older. The **Shaded Silver Persian** (sometimes also called the Pewter Persian) is like the Chinchilla but with much darker tipping. Both types can be born in the same litter and the difficulty of deciding which was which led to the separation into a separate breed being dropped in Britain, but a similar type, the **Pewter Longhair** has now been provisionally recognized there. Unlike the Chinchilla and the

Left: A Dilute Calico Persian.

Below: The lining around the Chinchilla's eyes and nose sets off its dazzling coat.

Right: The Shaded Cameo is the red version of the Shaded Silver Persian.

Left: The Shaded Silver Persian has darker tipping to its fur than does the Chinchilla.

American cat it has orange or copper eyes.

The Cameo cats are red versions of the Chinchilla and the Shaded Silver. The palest is the **Shell Cameo** (or Red Chinchilla) with light red tips to the topcoat. Its ear tufts and chest are white and its nose leather, eye rims and paw pads are rose pink. The **Shaded Cameo** (or Red Shaded) is a slightly darker form. The **Smoke Cameo** or Red Smoke (sometimes also called the Cameo Red) is the darkest. It is so heavily tipped that it may look like a solid red longhair until it moves, except that ruff and ear tufts are white. Some associations specify slightly different shades for the undercoat of the Smoke Cameo – from white or ivory to cream. In Britain a similar range of Cream Cameos has been provisionally recognized ranging from the **Shell Cream**, with a sparkling silver coat, lightly diluted with cream, and pink nose and paw pads, to the **Shaded** with even shading giving it a cream mantle, the **Cream Smoke** with a cream body shading to white on side and flanks and a cream mask and feet, and the **Blue-cream Cameo** with blue and cream tipping softly intermingled, and either pink or blue, or both, in nose leather and paw pads. All the Cameos have deep orange or copper eyes.

Above: A Shaded Golden Chinchilla.

Another recent, and very rare, version of the Chinchilla is the **Chinchilla Golden**, which has a warm cream undercoat with the head, back, sides and tail tipped seal brown and the rose-coloured leather and lips and the emerald eyes outlined in brown. A more heavily tipped form is known as the **Shaded Golden**.

Left: A Tortiepoint Colourpoint (Himalayan).

Smoke Longhairs have a white undercoat but instead of the solid black topcoat of the shorthair smokes their topcoat is very heavily tipped with black. It is darkest on the back, head and feet and shades down the sides. The face fur is black almost to the roots but the ruff and the ear tufts look silver. Nose leather and paw pads are black. The Blue Smoke is similar except that the Topcoat tipping is of blue and the nose leather and paw pads are blue.

Colourpoint (Himalayan)

The Himalayan breed of North America, known as the Colourpoint in Britain [not to be confused with the American Colorpoint, see page 68], is not classed with the Persians, although it is of identical type. It was deliberately created to transfer the point pattern of the Siamese coat to a typical Persian. First recognized in Britain, where the Seal (with dark brown points) and Blue were the first colours established, and chocolate, lilac, red, cream, tortoiseshell, blue-cream, chocolate-cream and lilac-cream points are now accepted, American recognition followed under the name Himalayan. In America the tortoiseshell points may be made up of seal, cream, blue or lilac combined with red and cream as well as the conventional black, red and cream and red; lilac, chocolate and seal lynx-point are also known. All of this breed have blue eyes.

Below: A Smoke Longhair.

Above: The Birman is easily distinguishable by its white paws.

Opposite, top: The Maine Coon has a sharper head than the Persian-type longhaired cats.

Birman

At a quick glance the Birman looks like the Himalayan, but a closer look shows that it differs in many ways, although it has the same Siamese points of colour on the face, ears, tail and paws. It is a quite independent breed and has no Persian-type longhairs in its ancestry. It is said to have been long established in south-east Asia and when first introduced to the west via France was known as the Sacred Cat of Burma. It has a long but fairly stocky body with a broad, rounded head, unlike that of either the Siamese or the Persian. Its nose is longer than a Persian's, so are its tail and legs, and its ears are larger. Its long silky fur tends to curl on its stomach and forms a ruff around its neck. The tail fur forms a long silky plume rather than the bush of the Persian.

European and American standards differ slightly in their requirements for the coat. In the Seal the ground colour in North America should be a pale fawn to cream – although it is claimed that cats with pure blood-lines have a golden halo to the whole back of the coat, reflecting the legend told about the breed in which a temple cat was suddenly transformed when a priest died in defending his temple against attack. In Europe a golden look is definitely expected, which the British standard describes as 'clear, pale beige with a slightly golden hue'. This cat's markings differ from those of the Siamese and the Himalayan in that the paws are white, as though the cat had stepped into a saucer of milk, with the white 'gloves' ascending up the back of the hind legs to end in a point. The Seal has pink paws pads and nose leather

(not as in the Siamese). Blue Point is also recognized on both sides of the Atlantic and in America Chocolate and Lilac as well. All Birmans have blue eyes.

Ragdoll

This is a very unusual American breed that looks just like the Birman in its original form, although it tends to have a heavier body, broader head and thicker fur. The original breeder found that a litter of kittens born to a cat that had been injured by a motorcar were relaxed and limp, flopping just like a child's ragdoll. These cats do not appear to have a normal nervous system, for it is claimed that they do not react to pain– which makes caring for them a great responsibility, for they consequently give little indication of injury or illness. They are placid and seem to have little sense of fear or danger. The original breeder described them as 'the closest one can get to a real live baby and still have an animal'. Some American associations now recognize parti-colored and colorpoint varieties as well as the original Birman-like 'mitted' type. They are not recognized in Britain and it is extremely unlikely that the development of a cat so disadvantaged would be encouraged in Europe. The Ragdoll's appeal seems to be to people who want a cat without the qualities of a cat.

Maine Coon

This long-established American breed is in rugged contrast to the Ragdolls. Its name comes from the old belief that it was the result of matings between cats brought over from Europe by early colonists and native American racoons – a cross-generic coupling which is not biologically possible. In some ways they resemble the American Shorthair and in others the Angora and they probably arose from crossing between the shorthaired cats taken to America by early settlers from Europe and Angoras introduced by later voyagers. They are often large cats, weighing as much as 30 lbs (13.5 kg), but nevertheless have quite delicate-looking faces with high cheekbones, a long nose with little or no break, slightly slanting oval eyes and large upright ears which are pointed at the tips. They are long in the body, tail and neck with none of the cobby, low-slung look of the Persian, and their fur is not so long. These cats are thought to have been feral in the New England countryside and rigorous east-coast winters produced a sturdy cat with a rugged, heavy coat. It is fairly short on the shoulders, becoming longer towards the tail and ending in shaggy breeches around the flanks. It becomes longer at the sides towards the stomach. The tail fur is full and long and there is a frontal ruff ranging from the base of the ears down over the chest. The base of the ears and their tips are tufted. The topcoat can get tangled but there is not much undercoat, which makes the breed easy to groom. The fur can be a wide range of colours: white, black, blue, cream, all the tabbies, tortoiseshell, tortoiseshell and white, calico, blue-cream and parti-color, and also tabby and white – a coat not recognized in any other pedigree breed, except in the tabby-point form of the Siamese or the tabby torties. Nose leather and paw pads should match the fur but the eyes may be any shade of green, gold or copper.

Turkish Cat

First recognized in Britain as the Turkish Van, this is a naturally occuring type indigenous to the area around Lake Van in Turkey. It is somewhat similar to the Angora [see page 48] which also comes from Turkey. It has a long, sturdy body with medium-length legs, rounded feet and a medium-length tail. The head is wedge-shaped, though shorter than in foreign-type cats, with a long nose. The large ears are upright and set close together and the eyes are large and round.

The Turkish Cat has long silky fur with no woolly undercoat and carries a full, well-furnished tail. The coat is chalky white, except for the tail, which is auburn with faint darker rings, and there are auburn markings on the face which extend from the base of the ears,

Right: The Balinese is a longhaired type of Siamese and has all the other characteristics of a Siamese cat.

Below: This Turkish Cat kitten will have a full luxuriant tail when it grows up.

leaving a white blaze on the forehead, and the ears themselves white. Some cats have auburn markings on the body but restriction to face and tail is preferred. Nose leather, paw pads and the insides of the ears are pink, as are the rims around the eyes.

Similar Turkish Cats of different colours have also been taken to Europe from other Turkish provinces – some are found in Sweden – but these auburn and white cats from Van are the only recognized breed at present, apart from the Angora. Males, in particular, are very hardy. In their homeland they have to cope with snow for half the year. They have shown an aptitude, even a fondness, for swimming, which has earned them the nickname 'Swimming Cats'.

Somali

This is a longhaired version of the Abyssinian cat [see page 72] and has exactly the same physique – a long, lithe body with a thick-based, tapering tail and a wedge-shaped but slightly rounded head with large pointed ears, and green or gold almond-shaped eyes. The fur is ticked along its length, and there are lines of darker colour around the eyes and on the forehead. It is long, soft and silky with a generous ruff and breeches on the hindparts. The ears have tufts at their tips and growing from them horizontally, and the tail is a generous plume. Both a Ruddy and a Red form are recognized in America and by some European clubs but do not have breen status in Britain.

Balinese

This is a longhaired version of the Siamese [see page 64] which retains all the Siamese characteristics of body shape; long legs and tail with a wedge-shaped head and large pointed ears – almost the opposite of the Persian – and the blue eyes and point markings of the coat. They have developed from the occasional mutant longhair born to a Siamese, not from deliberate cross-breeding with longhaired cats. At first Siamese breeders were unhappy to find such kittens in their litters but they were eventually recognized as beautiful cats in their own right and are now an official breed in America and becoming established in Britain. They retain all the delightful personality of the Siamese.

Cymric (Longhaired Manx)

Cymric – which means Welsh – is the Canadian name for this cat which is known in the United States as the Longhaired Manx. This is identical to its original shorthaired form [see page 46] in everything except the fur, which is softer as well as longer than the original Manx coat. It is of only medium length, not as long as that of most other longhaired cats.

Foreign Shorthairs

The Foreign Shorthair group of breeds used to be known as oriental cats, and still are by many people, especially in the United States. Some of these varieties probably did originate in the east but their name does not indicate their origin – rather that they all belong to a specific type with long, lean bodies, fine bones, long legs and tails, wedge-shaped heads rather than round ones, and short, sleek fur.

The Siamese is probably the most popular and certainly the most widely known to the general public. In general the other breeds share many of its characteristics, although there are distinct differences which can be easily observed.

The Seal Point was the first of the Siamese cats to be recognized.

Siamese

Pictures of Siamese cats and verses about them, which are thought to date from the Ayudha period, indicate that the *Vichien Mas*, the Seal Point Siamese, was already established in Thailand 400 years ago. The Siamese is not the common cat of Thailand – you are far more likely to see them in British homes than to encounter one in Bangkok – but it appears to have been a special pet of the court. The first of the breed taken to Europe in 1884 were apparently presents from the royal family and they were at first known as the Royal Cats of Siam. Their characteristic pattern was first noted by a European in a cat seen near the Caspian Sea in 1794. It was born of a black cat and may have been a chance mutation. It is not known where the type first developed but it is generally accepted that it had an eastern origin, perhaps in China. One Victorian 'expert' claimed that it was 'derived from a cross between the Sacred Cat of Burma [see page 60] and the Annamite cats that were introduced into . . . the Empire of Khmer'.

The breed was rapidly established in Britain and the Siamese Cat Society of America was founded in 1909.

Blue Point owners have claimed that this variety is the most gentle and affectionate of the Siamese.

The Royal Cat of Siam, as seen at cat shows at the beginning of this century, was a heavier cat than the required type today. It often had a kink in the tail and its eyes were frequently crossed – both features which would now be considered defects.

The modern Siamese should be a svelte, medium-sized cat with a long body, slim legs and small oval feet. Its head should narrow in straight lines to a fine muzzle, giving a straight profile. The ears are large, wide at the base and pointed at the tip. The eyes are almond-shaped, sloping upwards and outwards. Their colour should be a clear, deep blue – the British standard describes it as a bright, vivid blue, except for the lilac in which a lighter (but not pale) colour is described. The fur is short, fine textured and lies close to the body, giving a very sleek coat. In winter it may grow a little longer.

All varieties of Siamese have a pale body with a contrasting mask and points of darker fur. This darker colour extends over the feet and lower part of the legs, the whole length of the tail and the ears. On the face it spreads outwards from the nose, extending beyond the eyes and is joined to the base of the ears by narrow pencil lines of colour. As Siamese cats age their backs become darker and there may be a gradual extension of colour over both face and body, but the contrast is still clearly visible. The point pattern is a genetic dilution of colour – the original, and best known Siamese, the Seal Point, actually has points which are a dilute form of black.

Siamese are now recognized in Britain and America in a variety of colours: Seal, Blue, Chocolate and Lilac. In Britain Tabby Point, Red Point, Cream Point and Tortie Point are also recognized but most American associations class these colours separately as Colorpoint Shorthairs [see page 68]. Kittens are born with rather fluffy white coats that give no indication of their adult markings. The first sign is usually a darkening patch around the nose and points then become more and more defined as the kitten gets older, although the pencilling between the mask and ears may not develop until the cat is fully adult.

Seal Point cats have a cream body colour which shades from

Above: The Lilac Point Siamese was originally known as the Frost Point in North America.

Left: A Red Point Siamese. Red Points still show traces of a tabby pattern in their points.

Right: Tortie Point Siamese are produced when Red Points mate with Seal Point Siamese, but they are always female so they must be mated to other colours.

almost white on the belly to pale warm fawn on the back with points, nose leather and paw pads a really dark brown. **Blue Point,** the second colour to gain recognition, has a basic colour of glacial white, shading to a light blue on the back. Its points are a darker, cold-toned blue. **Chocolate Points,** originally rejected as poorly-coloured Seal Points (although, in fact, they are genetically quite different), were not recognized until half a century after the seal and blue. The coat is ivory in colour with any shading present the colour of the points, which should be milk chocolate in tone. Kittens tend to develop their points more slowly than the first two varieties and those which have a complete mask when young frequently become darker than desirable in a show cat by the time they are mature. The **Lilac Point,** or Frost Point as it was originally called and is still known in some associations, carries recessive genes for both blue and chocolate. Its coat is a milky or glacial off-white (magnolia, the British standard calls it) with points of pinkish-grey. In Britain nose leather and paw pads are described as faded lilac but one American association asks for lilac pink and another for 'translucent old lilac' nose leather and 'cold pink' paw pads. The American standards also require the same deep blue eyes as in the other colour varieties, although in Britain they may be of lighter blue. **Red Point Siamese** have a white coat, shading, if at all, to apricot on the back and with reddish-gold points. Nose leather should be pink. The **Cream Point** has a white coat shading to the very palest cream, with cream markings and pink nose leather. In both Red and Cream Points some tabby markings frequently still persist on the points and are not yet considered serious faults.

Tortie Point Siamese have their points patched in red and cream mixed with seal, blue, chocolate or lilac, the nose leather matching whichever of those basic colours is present as described above. **Tabby Points,** also known as **Lynx Point** in America, may have their points tabby-marked in seal, blue, chocolate, lilac or any of the tortoiseshell variations. There should be broken horizontal stripes on the legs, with the back of the hind legs solid

colour, and the tail should have clearly defined rings with a solid tip. The mask should have clear tabby stripes, especially around the eyes and nose, and the skin around the eyes should be dark rimmed to match the points colour and the whisker pads darkly spotted. Tortie Tabby Points should have mottled ears but in all the other tabbies the ears should be a solid colour except for a faint mark on the back – as though someone had pressed a thumb there. Nose leather should either conform to the standard for the tabby colour or be pink. Tortie Tabbies should have mottled paw pads.

Top: Tabby Point Siamese. Male Siamese can be very attentive fathers. Siamese kittens are quite fluffy when they are small.

Above: The Foreign White (White Oriental Shorthair) is a Siamese in which the point pattern has disappeared.

Colorpoint Shorthair

This is the name which several American associations give to the more recent colour variations of the Siamese which in Britain are classed as full Siamese and described above. They may be Lynx Point (Tabby Point) in seal, blue, chocolate or lilac; Red Lynx Point (because the red still carried some tabby markings) and Seal Tortie Point, Blue-cream Tortie Point, Chocolate-cream Tortie Point and Lilac-cream Tortie Point. This group should not be confused with the breed known in Britain as the Colourpoint, which is called the Himalayan in North America [see page 59].

Foreign White

Imagine a pure white Siamese without any mask or points and you have the Foreign White. It is a cat in which the genetic coding that produces the Siamese points has become so recessive that they have been removed altogether. It has pink nose leather and pink paw pads but it is not albino and its eyes are a brilliant blue. In America this type is grouped with the Oriental Shorthairs [see page 69].

Foreign Black

This is the British name for a Siamese type of cat in which the genetic coding has produced a solid black. The eyes are different too – they are green, not blue. Nose leather and paw pads are black. The equivalent cat is known in North America as the Ebony Oriental Shorthair [see page 69].

Foreign Lilac

Another cat of the Siamese type (known in America as the Lavender Oriental Shorthair), this cat has recessive genes for the dilution of pattern and recessive genes for chocolate and blue which together produce the lilac pattern overall – a frost grey with a pinkish tone. Nose leather and paw pads are pinkish and the eyes a vivid green.

Oriental Shorthairs

All these cats are identical to the Siamese except in their hair colouring, which is self-coloured without any mask or points. They include the cats which the British know as the Foreign White, Foreign Black (the Ebony in North America) and the Foreign Lilac (Lavender) and also included are a whole range of colours not yet recognized in Britain: Blue, Chestnut, Red, Cream, Cameo, Silver, Cameo Smoke, Chestnut Smoke, Blue Smoke, Ebony Smoke; and classic and mackerel, ticked and spotted tabbies in ebony, blue, chestnut, lavender, red, cream, silver,

Below: The Foreign Lilac (Lavender Oriental Shorthair) is another green-eyed oriental – in America they may also be amber-eyed.
Bottom: The Foreign Black (Ebony Oriental Shorthair) has green eyes, although it is of Siamese type.

cameo, tortoiseshell, blue-cream, chestnut tortie and lavender-cream. Their eyes may be either green or amber, except for the White, which can have blue or green eyes (but must not be odd-eyed). It has been suggested that they do not have such harsh voices as most Siamese.

In Britain 'Oriental' is used as the prefix only for the non-solid colours of foreign type: tabby, spotted [see page 73] tortoiseshell and smoke – self-colours using the prefix 'Foreign' described above.

Havana (Havana Brown)

This breed is another with Siamese conformation and was developed in Britain from the Chocolate Siamese with some crossbreeding to both Black Shorthairs and Russian Blues. For a time its name was changed to Chestnut Foreign Shorthair, but has now been re-established as the Havana. It has a rich chestnut brown coat which is slightly darker than the chocolate of its ancestors. Nose leather is rose pink and the eyes are dark green.

Breeding of Havana to Havana has failed to maintain the foreign conformation so occasional crosses back to the Siamese have been used in Britain to maintain the type. The first Havanas in America were imports from Britain but the American strain, known as the Havana Brown, was not crossed back to Siamese and in America it has a more rounded muzzle, rounded tips to the ears, a distinct stop level with the eyes and a slight break behind the whiskers. Because it is now not of full Siamese type it is not included among the Colorpoint Shorthairs

Korat

This cat comes from Thailand where it is more frequently found than the Siamese. It has been known there for centuries under the name *Si-Sawat*. *Sawat* means good luck or prosperity and the people of the Korat plateau, from which it takes its name, prize it as a bringer of good fortune. It is a sturdy and muscular cat of medium size with shorter legs than the Siamese, oval paws and a medium-length tail that is heavy at the base and tapers to a rounded tip. It has a large, flat forehead and a strong, but not sharply pointed, muzzle, giving a rather heart-shaped face. In profile the nose has a slightly downward curve and there is a slight stop between nose and forehead. The ears are large and set high on the head, with a flaring base and rounded tips. The

Above: The Havana is a sleek and glossy cat. Breeders have commented that Havanas enjoy playing in the snow. Strong summer sun can bleach their fur, making the tail especially gingery.

Left: The Korat has a long history in Thailand where the males are admired as fearless fighters, though they make gentle and responsive pets.

Opposite, top: This Russian Blue tom has a beautiful coat but his eyes should be a more vivid green to match the standard.

large eyes are spaced well apart and although round when fully open appear to have an oriental slant when shut or partly closed. From kitten blue they change first to amber and then to a luminous green, often with a golden cast, which may not be achieved until the cat is two years old.

The Korat's coat is a silvery blue all over, each hair being tipped with silver. This silver tipping develops during kittenhood and adolescence until the cat is about two. The coat is fine and glossy, short to medium in length and lies close to the body. It is inclined to break along the spine as the cat moves and the silver sheen is greatest where the hair is shortest. An old Thai poem describes its fur as 'smooth with roots like clouds and tips like silver' and says its 'eyes shine like dewdrops on a lotus leaf'. Korats were rarely seen outside Thailand before 1959, when a pair was taken to America, but they are now becoming increasingly better known on both sides of the Atlantic.

Russian Blue

Another all-blue cat is the Russian Blue, which is also one of the earliest known cats of foreign type if we are to identify it with the cats known as Archangel Blues, said to have been imported into England by Elizabethan sailors returning from the Russian Arctic port. At one time this type became very confused with the British Blue, and the two types competed together, but separate classes were established in the 1920s. Later, Siamese blood was introduced which intensified the foreign look but this trend has since been reversed. In Britain the Russian Blue still looks rather more oriental than the American type but both have long and graceful bodies with long legs and small oval feet and fairly long, tapering tails. The wedge-shaped head is shortish with a straight nose, strong chin and prominent whisker pads. In Britain the ears should be large and pointed, wide at the base and set vertically on the head, but in North America they are set closer and are not so pointed. The almond-shaped eyes are vivid green.

The Russian Blue has a soft, thick, double coat which is even and clear blue throughout. In America lighter shades are preferred and guard hairs should be tipped with silver. In Britain nose leather and paw pads are blue, in America the nose is slate-grey and the paw pads lavender pink or mauve.

Abyssinian

In 1868 a cat of this type was taken home to England from Ethiopia by a party of British soldiers and it has been suggested that this breed are direct descendants from the cats of ancient Egypt, but it has also been suggested that the breed owes its origin much more to a carefully regulated breeding programme on the part of British breeders who wanted to create a cat of the ancient type. The agouti coat, with each hair having bands of colour along its length, is genetically a form of tabby and can occur in other litters, but it is also shared by one of the forms of the African Wild Cat.

The Abyssinian is an elegant, medium-sized cat with a firm, muscular body and tapering tail, which are both fairly long. It has slim legs and oval feet. Its head is wedge-shaped but quite broad and gently rounded without flat planes. There is a slight indentation on either side of the muzzle which is not pointed, a slight rise from the bridge of the nose to the forehead and large, broad-based ears, preferably with tufts of hair at their gently pointed tips. The large, almond-shaped eyes, with an oriental slant, may be amber, hazel or green.

Each hair of the short, fine fur is striped with two or three bands of alternating dark and light colour, giving an overall tone that ranges from pale on the underside and chest to darker on the back, with dark fur up the hind legs and a dark tip to the tail, but there must be no barring or stripes nor any white patches anywhere. There is a line of darker colour around the eyes and dark lines extend from the eyes over the forehead, these both being strikingly set off against lighter-coloured fur.

The **Usual or Ruddy Abyssinian,** the original variety, is a rich golden grown ticked with black, with an undercoat of rich apricot or orange-red. Tail tip, paw pads and the back of the hind legs are black, nose leather brick red. There is also a **Sorrel (or Red) Abyssinian** with deep apricot undercoat and a body colour of copper red ticked with chocolate. Its nose leather and paw pads are pink. A **Blue Abyssinian** with a pale cream undercoat and blue-grey topcoat with deeper steel blue, has been recognized and Abyssinians have also been produced in chocolate, lilac, cream and silver.

Egyptian Mau

At the end of 1956 a spotted cat acquired in Cairo and two of her kittens were imported into the United States. The kittens had been raised in Rome, sired by another Egyptian cat, and they all looked very like the spotted cats seen in some ancient Egyptian paintings. As with the Abyssinians, it has been suggested that this type of cat is descended from a form of *Felis lybica*. Careful breeding in America produced clear spotting and the type was recognized as a new breed under the name Egyptian Mau. *Mau* is the ancient Egyptian word for cat, and also meant 'to see'. These cats are not as foreign looking as the Siamese and about halfway between the foreign and shorthair types. Their graceful body is medium long with a medium-long tail, thick at the base and tapering to the tip. The hind legs are longer than the front and the feet are small and dainty. The head is a modified, slightly-rounded wedge-shape with no flat planes, brow, cheek and profile all showing a gentle contour. The large, alert ears are broad at the base and slightly pointed. Large, almond-shaped eyes slope slightly upwards to the ears.

The fine silky fur is dense and long enough to accommodate two or more bands of ticking. The cat's forehead has a distinct M mark and lines between the ears continue down the neck and break into elongated spots along the spine, forming a stripe along the top of the tail, which is also ringed with a dark tip. There are necklaces across the chest, spotting over the body and barring on the legs. Three colour forms have been recognized. The **Silver** has a silver base coat with charcoal markings, with nose, lips and eyes outlined in black, black paw pads and brick red nose leather. The **Bronze** has dark brown markings on a bronze ground with outlining in brown with black or dark brown pads and a brick red nose. The **Smoke,** with dark charcoal grey markings on a silver undercoat, has black outlining, pads and nose. Some associations also recognize a **Pewter** Mau with a pale fawn ground colour, each hair ticked with silver and beige and with black tipping. Nose, lips and eyes are outlined in dark brown. Nose leather is brick red and paw pads charcoal or dark brown.

Oriental Spotted Tabby

During the development of the Tabby Point Siamese in Britain kittens appeared which, like the Mau, resembled the spotted cats of ancient Egypt. From them Angela Sayer chose a female to commence a breeding programme to recreate the Egyptian form. Some Havana blood was introduced to produce a bronze coloration and back crosses to Siamese helped to maintain the type. An extremely beautiful cat, it has a clearly shaped scarab between the ears, looking like the symbol of the sacred Egyptian beetle which appears on so many ancient amulets. However, this cat is definitely of Siamese type, unlike the American-bred Mau, and the British Governing body would not permit its registration as an Egyptian Mau. It has consequently been recognized as the Oriental Spotted Tabby.

Burmese

The whole Burmese breed had its origin in one female cat which an American traveller to Burma took back home with him to San Francisco. She looked like a dark Siamese and when mated to a Siamese some of the kittens in the litter looked just like herself. A carefully managed breeding programme eventually gained recognition for this dark, glossy-coated oriental.

Except in young cats, in which the point pattern of the Siamese is still discernible, it is difficult to tell some purebred Burmese from hybrid cats and in 1947, after suggestions that hybrids were being shown and sold as pure Burmese,

Above: A Sorrel Abyssinian.

Left: A Brown Burmese.

recognition was withdrawn. In the period before recognition was restored in 1953 some Burmese were sent to England and the breed established there. The British strain has a more Siamese type than is acceptable in America, although both are distinctly different cats from the extreme oriental and from the cobby shorthairs.

The Burmese is of medium length with a heavy, muscular build and a weight that its appearance does not suggest. The chest is strong and rounded, the back is straight and the medium length tail tapers only slightly to its rounded tip. The head tapers to a short, blunt wedge, is slightly rounded on top with full, wide cheeks, a distinct nose break and a strong lower jaw. The forward-tilting ears are slightly rounded at their tips and the large, wide-set eyes are almost round in America, and in Britain have an oriental slant only on the top with a rounded lower edge. The British cat has oval feet, like the Siamese, but in America they must be round.

In America four colour varieties are recognized, although some people claim that the original dark brown, or Sable, is the only true Burmese. These four are **Sable,** with rich brown nose leather and paw pads; **Champagne,** with the coat a rich warm honey-beige, shading to a lighter tone on the chest and underparts and with darker shading on the face and ears permitted, nose leather a light

Right: A Lilac Burmese.

Below: A Cream Burmese.

warm brown and paw pads pale pink; **Blue,** again with a lighter colour on the chest and underparts and seasonal fawn overtones appearing in the rich blue, with nose and pads slate grey tinged with pink; and **Platinum,** a pale silvery-grey which also seasonally has fawn overtones with lavender pink nose and pads. All four colour varieties have golden eyes.

Champagne and Platinum are not known as such in Britain but many other colours are recognized. The **Chocolate** Burmese has a warm milk chocolate coat with brown nose leather and paw pads of brick pink shading to chocolate. The **Lilac** has a pale dove-grey coat with a pinkish tinge, lavender pink nose and pads (the pads being pink in kittens). **Red** is light tangerine with the ears distinctly darker than the back and pink nose and pads. Slight tabby markings are permitted on the face of the Red. The **Cream** has a rich cream coat when adult, with darker ears, and may also show some slight tabby markings. Its paw pads and nose leather are pink. The **Tortoiseshell** may have plain or blotched brown and pink nose and pads. The **Blue-cream** has a well-mixed coat with plain or blotched, blue and pink nose and pads.

Breeders suggest that Burmese are happiest when kept with others of their own breed, which, like most orientals, enjoy company and involvement with humans.

Tonkinese

This is an American hybrid breed created by crossing the Siamese and the Burmese. In Britain the difference between the conformation of the breeds would not have been sufficient to develop a distinct type but the American cat can be distinguished by its tapering tail, dainty oval paws and almond-shaped, slightly oriental eyes. The head is a slightly rounded wedge with a rise from the bridge of the nose to the forehead. The Siamese point pattern still shows in the coat, gently merging into the body colour. The eyes are a rich blue-green and coat colours are Natural Mink, a warm brown with dark chocolate to sable points, and Honey Mink, a more reddish brown with reddish points. A rich chocolate brown, champagne and blue-grey have also been produced.

A Red Burmese. The darker colour hair on the ears can just be seen on the tips.

A naturally short-tailed cat, the Japanese Bobtail is a familiar sight in its country of origin.

Japanese Bobtail

This is a very individual breed and indigenous to Japan. It has been known there for hundreds of years and appears in many old Japanese paintings and woodblock prints. It is not properly grouped with the Foreign Shorthairs at all, for it is quite unlike them in type. It is long in body and more slender than the British and American Shorthairs, with slender muscular legs, the hind ones being longer than the forelegs. However, because it holds the hind legs bent when relaxed its back maintains a level line. It has a long, triangular head with gently curving sides, high cheekbones and a noticeable whisker break. The ears are large and upright and set fairly high on the head. The eyes are large, oval and set on a slant. Most noticeable, however, is the very short tail from which it gets its name. It is usually kinked which makes it look even shorter and with its thick covering of rather long, fine hair which grows in all directions, it can look something like a large tassel or pompom. The rest of the coat is of only medium length, soft and silky, and without a noticeable undercoat.

Japanese Bobtails come in all kinds of colours in Japan but the tricolour of white patched with black and red is considered lucky and is particularly favoured there. This and bi-colours of black and white, or red and white, tortoiseshell, and tortoiseshell and white, are all accepted by American associations.

The New Kitten or Cat

Plan to introduce a kitten or cat to its new home when you can be there to spend plenty of time with it. Do not collect it one evening and then go off to work next morning – and certainly do not just take it home and leave it on its own. If you are working and cannot take a holiday then collect it in the evening at the beginning of the weekend so that you can be around to give it plenty of reassurance and attention.

There are preparations and decisions which you must make in advance. You must decide upon some basic rules for you cannot expect to impose restrictions once the cat has got used to being allowed to do things – although you can abandon restrictions without problems. Decide where you are going to allow the cat to go: whether certain rooms are to be out of bounds, whether it is to be allowed to jump up on to furniture and other surfaces, and whether it is going to be allowed to sleep on your bed. You must prevent it from doing things which could be dangerous to it, or to any other animal or person, and you will not want it to damage your home or possessions. Decide where you are going to feed it, where to put its litter tray and where you want it to

Sharp claws can cause havoc to furniture, especially when kittens are having fun.

Opposite, top: A litter tray is essential for an indoor cat. Most kittens will have been taught to use one by their mothers.

Left: A few playthings make life much more fun for a kitten. But make sure toys are not stuffed with anything which could do harm if swallowed.

sleep (these can be changed later if they prove inconvenient but need planning ahead).

You will need to obtain a suitable litter tray and litter for the kitten to excrete in, even though you may later permit it to go outdoors. The tray should be about 3 in (5 cm) deep and about 12 x 18 in (30 x 45 cm). Inexpensive plastic trays are easily cleaned and disinfected. There are types available which have covers high enough to give a cat room inside but prevent all but the smallest amount of scattering of litter even by the most energetic scratcher upper. Commercially packaged litter, usually a type of fuller's earth, is odour and moisture absorbing, although quite expensive. If you have storage space large packs generally prove better value. If you use a small trowel or scoop to remove dry solid lumps you can make it go further. For even greater economy you can put a wad of newspaper in the tray and scatter a small quantity of litter on top. This will need changing frequently but will also use less litter. All cats will object to using a very soiled tray. Some people use sand, sawdust or ash but these generally tend to be messy, tread about the house, and become a smelly, soggy mass. Peat is a better possibility – it can be used later in the garden. Since it can retain germs after use by the cat it should be well-rotted in the garden compost heap where the high temperature of the decomposing rubbish will kill them off.

It is advisable, especially for a cat that is to stay largely indoors, to have a scratching post or block on which the claws can be exercised. These are sold by pet stores, or you can make one by covering a post or block of wood with coarse hessian, old carpet or other tough fabric – or you might use a natural splinter-free log. It is a good idea to choose something different from other surfaces in the house so that it is clearly differentiated by texture as well as place. An alternative would be to sacrifice a piece of furniture which the cat can tear to pieces!

A cat bed does not have to be a special basket, although some comfortable ones are sold. A box padded with newspaper (easily replaced) and covered with a piece of blanket will serve well and a cardboard box can also be easily changed if it gets soiled. Most traditional beds used to be made of woven wicker but modern ones of fibreglass and plastic are more hygienic. Choose a place for the bed that is out of draughts (bend down and check) and will not be continually disturbed by household coming and going. A cat may choose some other place to sleep – and you may decide to let it do so – but a new kitten or a cat in a new home will need a base to call its own.

A hot-water bottle under the blanket can be used to replace the warmth that a kitten has been used to getting from curling up with its mother and litter mates and a loudly ticking clock, such as a wind-up alarm clock, tucked in beside it, will give a reassuring regular sound like the beating of its mother's heart. If you do use an alarm clock make sure that the alarm is *not* wound for if it should go off it would give the kitten a terrible fright! Similarly do not let a hot-water bottle go cold, or it will have a reverse effect. Heating pads, either metal ones or miniature electric blankets, are sold for pet beds and are probably a good way of encouraging a cat not to choose some other spot to sleep – but they must be entirely safe and waterproof.

Some playthings will also be a sensible addition. They do not have to be shop-bought toys, although some amusing ones are available. Avoid toys that have any sharp edges or which are stuffed with cotton wool or kapok, which the kitten might ingest. A piece of string, an empty cotton reel (and the one tied to the other), stiff paper to make a crumpled ball, a few sheets of newspaper to hide beneath, will cost you nothing and all make excellent playthings. A table-tennis ball will also give lots of fun and is unlikely to do any damage to kitten or house.

Special food and water bowls are not strictly necessary, although

The warm top of a solid fuel stove may be a cosy place to curl up – but cats should be taught to keep away from electric and gas cookers, and if this stove is hot enough to simmer a kettle these kittens could easily burn their paws.

Outdoor cats can use a tree to exercise their claws.

it is wise to keep the dishes used separate from your family tableware. However, inexpensive plastic dishes are available which are shaped to make them difficult to tip over and they will help reduce the risk of mess – although many cats insist on dragging large pieces of food out on to the floor. One more expensive type of feeder has a cover to keep flies and dirt off the food. Newspaper which can be frequently changed or a sheet of thick plastic which can be easily cleaned will save food spills from damaging your floor covering.

Initially you should follow the exact diet which a kitten or cat has been used to eating. Ask the breeder or previous owner for a breakdown of food and feeding times. A kitten of eight or nine weeks should be fully weaned and eating four varied meals a day. They should include meat – an all fish diet can lead to skin disorders (and some cats may reject fish altogether) – and most kittens will enjoy a little breakfast cereal mixed in with their food, or some rice pudding mixed with a little evaporated milk. Canned and dried foods can be gradually introduced when the cat is older [see page 89] and any transition to a different diet should be introduced gradually.

A sturdy carrying box or basket is essential for collecting your new pet. For a very short journey a closed-up cardboard box with breathing holes cut in it will serve. Specially designed cardboard carriers approved by the RSPCA are sold by some veterinary surgeons and cat homes, as well as being stocked by pet stores. These will not stand frequent usage and the efforts of intrepid adult cats to get out, so a durable basket of wicker, wire or fibreglass is a worthwhile investment. Wicker is the traditional material but it is not so easy to clean and disinfect. Plastic-coated wire is easy to clean but the basket should be lined with old newspapers (and perhaps a piece of blanket) to give the cat a firmer base to lie on and some protection from cold in cool weather, especially if the cat is to be carried in the open or on public transport. A lining of newspaper around the sides may also keep out inquisitive fingers or other animals' paws as well as draughts. It is easier to lift an uncooperative cat in and out of a top-opening basket but many are designed to open at one end.

Unless your cat is never to be allowed to go outdoors you also need a collar and name tag, or cylinder, so that if it should ever get lost or into difficulties you can easily be traced. The collar must be one specially made for cats, with an elasticated section which will stretch to allow the cat to wriggle free if the collar should become hooked on to a twig or nail. The identity disc should carry your name, address and telephone number. The cylinder tag carries a rolled-up piece of paper, so if you frequently travel with the cat – to a weekend home for instance, and on holidays – you can change the roll of paper and the address to the appropriate location. A lead which snaps on to the collar will give you a means of controlling the cat's movements (always useful when travelling or going to the vet), even if you do not attempt to take the cat for walks on the lead.

Some people prefer a harness to a collar for leading and controlling a cat. This transfers any tug from the neck to the body but, while a collar can be opened up by another

Opposite, top: Do not *use family pans and dishes for feeding your pets, keep some for cat use only.*

Opposite, bottom: It is much easier to lift a reluctant cat out of a top-opening carrier.

Above: A collar with an elastic section will allow your cat to wriggle free if it gets caught up. It should carry an identity disc or a cylinder tag.

hole on the buckle as the kitten grows, harnesses are not usually so flexible and you will probably have to change a harness as the cat gets bigger.

It is a good idea, if you already have a cat or dog in the house, to take with you either a little soiled cat litter or a blanket or other material well-impregnated with the established cat or dog's smell, when you set off to collect the new cat or kitten. If you rub the litter or the blanket on the new cat you will transfer some of the scent of the established pet, which will then accept the newcomer more readily. Do this before you enter the house on your return or, if collecting the cat from only a short distance away, before you leave its previous home. This technique is also particularly useful if you have a young orphan kitten and want a lactating cat to accept it with its own litter.

If a new kitten is still with its mother the breeder will probably take her out of the room so that she

does not become upset by seeing the kitten leave. Make a fuss of your kitten and let it get thoroughly familiar with you. If you have already met and played with it it may even recognize your smell. When you are ready to leave put it securely in the basket and make it comfortable. Ensure that you have all the necessary documentation and information about diet and so on, and check that the cat is securely in its basket before you go outside. If you have a long journey it is often best for the travelling basket to be closed in and to ignore the kitten entirely. In that way it becomes bored and will go to sleep. If it wakes up you can talk to it to reassure it. On a very long journey, or if the cat is frightened,

Left: Kittens often appear to play quite roughly but their fur offers some protection from sharp claws and they are instinctively inhibited from doing serious harm to each other. Nevertheless you should beware of those sharp little claws.

Below: Established cats can sometimes be extremely jealous of new arrivals and they need to be given plenty of attention so that their noses are not put out of joint.

it may urinate – but a wad of newspaper will soak that up.

Try to arrange that an established cat or dog will not be able to see you or rush to greet you when you get home. If there is someone else in the house they could take it out or keep it occupied as you come in. This will enable the new arrival to be discovered in the house and not met as an intruder trying to enter the established animal's territory. When they meet do not try to restrain either party on a leash, this will only increase any possible antagonism. If you are lucky the new arrival will have recognized that it is on another's territory and be appropriately submissive. The scent which you have transferred to it will make it seem more acceptable, and if it is submissive it will not have to be treated as a threat.

It may at first be easier not to put the new cat's bed in the room which the other animal considers its main territory, although if they are later to share it, it should not be left too long before they are encouraged to do so, lest the separation becomes too well established.

Take the new animal into the place where it will have its bed and open the travelling basket after having first closed the door and all windows and other places where it might try to rush out, such as a chimney, which should be boarded up. Encourage the cat or kitten to come out and explore. Talk to it and stroke it, show it its litter tray. If it has been a long journey it will probably use it. It may make a careful investigation of the whole room. Accompany it as it explores this room, and the rest of its new home, but let it decide for itself whether somewhere is safe or not. When it seems reasonably secure you could welcome in an established cat or dog. It is important to treat the original pet as normal, and not to give the new cat more attention or affection, or you will make the old one jealous.

In most cases, after a little preliminary sniffing, circling and skirmishing the newcomer will be submissive and gain acceptance. Occasionally the older animal may be the more frightened and retreat, but a young animal will usually win it over. If they fight the kitten may try to get back into the protection of its basket. You may have to risk a scratch or two but eventually animals learn that they have to tolerate each other and they will usually become good friends.

Play games with the new kitten (involving other pets if they are about so that they do not get jealous) and when the kitten is tired and goes to sleep fill the hot-water bottle and lift the kitten gently into its bed – if it has not snuggled up there already. Cats sleep for about two-thirds of the time, and a young kitten needs a lot of sleep and should be allowed to rest undisturbed by inquisitive humans. At the end of the day, when you retire, make sure there is a new hot bottle and a ticking clock to comfort the new kitten.

Let the cat explore those parts of the house where it will be allowed to go but do not let it go outside until it has become really settled and familiar with its new home, which will probably take about a fortnight. Before you allow it out it is advisable to take it to the vet for a general check-up, and if a kitten has not already been inoculated against Panleukopenia this must be done before it is allowed out. The shots, which can be given from the age of six weeks, need time to take effect and build up resistance, so the cat must be kept indoors and away from any visiting cats for a week after they have been given.

When you decide to let the cat go out you should certainly go with it and might try keeping it on a lead at first, even if you do not wish to lead train it. If you live in a town or near a busy road it is unwise to let it out on the street but if you feel the risks from accident are slight you could fit a cat door, consisting of a flap which the cat can push open, so that it can come and go when it pleases. Most types can be fitted into a door panel or a piece of wood replacing a window pane; some can be set into a pane of glass. An alternative is to make a special hole in the wall. Some cat doors are held shut magnetically and only open when a cat wearing a matched magnet on its collar tries to pass – they are a way of keeping out other cats. Most cat flaps have a catch to keep them shut for times when you need to keep a cat indoors.

The indoor cat, used to a litter tray, will come in to excrete if not retrained when it is allowed to go outdoors. The simplest way is to carry the litter tray outside to somewhere in the garden which you do not mind the cat using as its toilet place. Continue to change the litter to make sure that is where the cat goes, then remove the tray but leave a little litter on the ground. If the cat happily continues to go there you can assume successful retraining. However, if the cat is shut in the house at all, it must be provided with a litter tray.

Some people always put a cat out at night. It is true that wild cats are nocturnal, or at least crepuscular, animals, but by domesticating it you have changed its life style. A farm cat which sleeps all day and hunts all night may make sense, and will have plenty of places to shelter from cold or wet weather, but a town cat is likely to be cold and miserable and runs a great risk of being run over, as well as being more likely to get into fights. It is therefore better to shut the cat in at night – and you will sleep more soundly too!

Top: Always make time to play with your cats.

Right: A cat flap will enable your cat to come and go as it pleases.

Caring For Your Cat

Feeding

A wild or feral cat is perfectly capable of looking after itself but a domestic animal lives in artificial circumstances. Its care is your responsibility. Most important is to see that it gets fed. Even a cat that is kept as a mouser will need a supplementary diet to be fit.

First, always ensure that there is a supply of clean, fresh water. You will often see a cat drinking from a garden pool, a saucepan in the sink, or even a puddle – but unless you can discover exactly what makes that source so tasty offer it fresh.

Second, never leave food down for long periods to become contaminated.

Third, wash dishes out carefully and rinse them free of soap or detergent. You may not notice the taste of detergent on your dishes but cats do. Never use any cleaner or disinfectant with a carbolic base on anything pertaining to your cat. Carbolic acid is dangerous for cats.

Cats cannot digest a lot of roughage, whether in the form of starch or green vegetables, they eat largely animal protein. In the wild they get minerals and trace elements from the stomach contents of their prey and these must be provided in other form. An adult needs about fifty calories per day per pound body weight. If you reckon about 30 gm per kilo (half an ounce per pound) you will be about right. A growing kitten or a pregnant cat will need rather more.

Above left: This is the correct way to hold a cat, supporting its weight . . .

Above: Never *hold a cat like this.*

Kittens up to the age of three months have only tiny stomachs, no bigger than a walnut, so their meals must be small and frequent. Some cats, mainly orientals, have difficulty in digesting milk, but as kittens seem to like it. Ordinary cows' milk is too dilute for a cat and often causes diarrhoea. Rich creamy milk is closer to cats' milk. There are special formula powdered milks available for young kittens but these are usually only necessary if you have to hand-feed to raise an orphan, or supplement the supply of a mother who cannot properly feed her litter. Canned, unsweetened evaporated milk seems acceptable to most kittens. It can be mixed with canned creamed rice. Some breeders beat an egg into each half pint of cows' milk to give it added strength.

At first feed a kitten exactly what its breeder gave it but you can then adapt to two or three meals a day of milk and rice or baby cereals, alternating with two of chopped-up meat or flaked fish. By four months this can be cut down to a breakfast of milk and cereal and an evening meal of meat or fish, with a snack of some kind at midday. At six months morning and evening meals alone suffice, and some cats will soon be happy with only a single evening meal, provided that it is a big one.

If you give fresh meat or fish you would be wise to add a supplement of calcium pills or bonemeal. If cats cannot or will not drink milk they particularly need another source of calcium. Some will grind up bones and many will enjoy gnawing on a big bone – but remember that cooked bones can be brittle, stewed ones can become soft. Small, splintery bones and sharp jagged ones should be removed, they can get wedged in the throat or pierce the intestines. Soft ones can get wedged on the incisors. Even with raw meat and fish do not take risks with bones.

If you cook the meat add yeast to replace the Vitamin B which is lost in cooking. An unchanging diet risks being deficient in some respect, so vary what you feed a cat. Liver will provide some of the necessary vitamins of A and E, but large quantities or serving it too often can cause bowel upsets.

Most cats have quite unusual things that they enjoy: green beans, asparagus, or mushrooms, to sherry and smoked salmon. It is

Left: Cats are contrary creatures and even when provided with water some prefer to find it for themselves.

perfectly all right to indulge your cat occasionally but never let it get faddy. If it refuses food that is perfectly sound let it go without – and do not serve a treat at the next meal! Once a cat gets hungry it is not likely to be so choosy and it will do it no harm to miss one meal. However, do not miss out meals just for your own convenience. Cats are creatures of routine and if you neglect them they will be disoriented.

Exactly what you feed your cat will depend upon your budget and on availability. Most proprietary cat foods are now formulated to give a balanced diet – but check the labelling or ask the manufacturers for details. Canned and dried foods and vacuum-packed moist foods are easy to store. Many pet shops also stock precooked prepared mixtures, some of which will keep for short periods. Always check how long they will stay fresh.

If you feed dried foods make sure that there is always plenty of water available and that the cat does drink it – insufficient water in conjunction with dried foods can lead to calculi and other painful urinary conditions developing, especially in neutered toms. If the cat seldom drinks water, feed the food moistened with water or milk.

Ring the changes with different kinds of canned food, some dried food, offal, fish and meat. As well as giving the cat variety this will also ensure that if a particular food is unavailable feeding will not be a problem.

If a cat can roam outdoors in gardens or countryside it will take the occasional snack of grass or other greenstuff, and an indoor cat should have its own supply of grass. Grow some in a pot, the type known as cocksfoot is usually liked. Eating grass provides roughage (like humans eating bran), and it also helps cats who swallow a lot of fur when washing to regurgitate the balls this forms.

Below: Grass plays a useful role in the diet of every cat.

Training

Discipline and consistency are the key to any animal training. Punishment plays no part but reward and encouragement are very important. Timing is a key factor too: there is no point in reproving a cat for doing something long after the event. Generally it will not connect the two – although a trained cat which has transgressed will probably be warily guilty for quite a while afterwards. The time to tell a cat off is when it is thinking of doing something or actually doing it. It is easy to tell when a cat is about to jump up on a table or to scratch a favourite chair. If it does jump simply lift or push it off again and tell it 'No!' or 'Bad cat!' Some people suggest sharply hitting the table behind the cat with a rolled-up newspaper – but while you are reaching for your newspaper the cat will probably be waiting to jump off again and think it has invented a splendid game to make you hit the table whenever it wants. If a cat reaches to scratch in the wrong place carry it to its scratching post and lift its paws against the post. Introduce the cat to the post in just that way – preferably when you see it wanting to scratch. It is not sharpening its claws, as many people think, but exercising the muscles and removing the old sheaths from the claws to uncover sharp new points beneath.

If a young kitten has any 'accidents' and does not use its litter tray do not rub its nose in the mess. If you are present simply pick the kitten up and place it in its tray. Then thoroughly clean up and disinfect the place so that no scent remains to suggest that this is a proper toilet area! Cats bruise easily and should never be struck in reproof. A light tap on the nose with one finger is enough, or at most a glancing blow on the end of the back – but vocal expression of displeasure will often be sufficient on its own. Show your pleasure when it does things right by stroking and speaking gently in approval. Tone of voice is very rapidly understood.

Where you allow your cat to go is your decision but it should certainly be taught not to jump up on to surfaces such as cookers and hotplates. Even if you do not mind when the cooker is cold it could seriously burn itself if the rings or plates are alight. Shelves and other places where ornaments are displayed, and surfaces where food is prepared should also be out of bounds. Cats can delicately pick their way among things without doing damage but they cannot see what is there before jumping from below.

Cats must not be allowed to play with electrical wiring. For general safety you will avoid unnecessary trailing cables between table lamps and other fittings and wall plugs but some are unavoidable. Pulling on them could bring a lamp down, chewing them or a claw penetrating their insulation could electrocute the cat. If a cat has plenty of other things to play with it will not play with wires once it has been taught not to do so. Never use lengths of electric cable for games or you may confuse the cat.

Many of the games that kittens play with their litter mates are practice for hunting and if a cat is kept largely indoors you should not only provide it with playthings but make time to play with

Above: Where you allow your cat to go is up to you.

Right: Teaching a cat to walk on a lead takes patience but will mean that you can take your cat with you almost anywhere.

it yourself in kittenhood and right through its life. Chasing a leaf or a cotton reel is one thing but a piece of string that is being pulled, or a ball of paper that is thrown are much more fun. Cats will invent their own games and encourage you to play them but do not take risks with claws, especially with young kittens whose claws are often sharper than you expect. Some cats used to a lot of human contact may retract their claws whenever they touch your skin, but even they may forget in the excitement of a game and tear your flesh.

Some cats make good retrievers and, like a dog with a stick or a ball, will bring back a ball of crumpled paper or other object which they can easily pick up in their teeth, eager for it to be thrown again. They love pouncing on or under sheets of newspaper, and also enjoy jumping into paper bags and cardboard boxes.

Cats usually learn their names very rapidly – even though they may choose to ignore them when you call. Use their names when stroking them, never when admonishing them. If mealtimes are regular they will usually come if called to eat, in fact they will probably be there waiting.

One of the hardest things to teach a cat is to walk on a lead. Orientals have gained a reputation for being more adaptable in this way but the number seen out walking does not suggest that success comes often. If training is started when a kitten is very young – before you would actually take it outside – perhaps you have more chance of succeeding. Kittens have a strong instinct to follow their mother and when they have left her you become a mother substitute. If a kitten follows you capitalise upon this trait. Before attaching a leather lead to the cat's collar use a light nylon cord or a piece of string. Once it has got used to having a lead and collar attached – and it may want to play with it for quite a time at first – try just letting it follow you as you hold the other end of the lead. If it does not exhibit this behaviour then hold the lead slack and call the kitten to you, taking up the slack in the lead as it approaches. Do this over a couple of days for a few minutes each time, then try walking backwards, then eventually try to get it to follow you on the lead. It may obstinately sit firm, but eventually it will walk a few steps. Praise it and do not expect more. Next day, or at least after a long interval, try again. Keep the lead slack until you are sure that the kitten is really used to it, then allow it to pull enough to restrain the cat. As with all training a few minutes each day will be much more effective than long sessions further apart. If the kitten really seems to hate walking on a lead then it is probably better to forget the whole idea.

If a cat has not learned to walk on a lead it is essential to have a basket to carry it in when going to the vet or on any other journey. Even if you travel in a car a cat should not be loose inside it. It can easily dash out when the door is opened, may try to climb through an open window and can easily cause an accident if it gets under the feet of the driver or otherwise in the way. If you have a companion in the back seat and a cat that enjoys looking at the view then, provided that it is restrained on a leash, it could be allowed out – indeed this is even possible on public transport if you have a well-behaved cat, but there is always a risk that if something unexpected should frighten it a cat will probably try to dash for cover.

Above: A travelling box or basket is essential for journeys.

Holidays

Some people find that their cats will happily adapt to being in new surroundings and take them on holiday with them. This should only be risked if the cat can either be kept indoors or if it is totally reliable at coming when called or you may find it wandering and not back when you wish to leave and then straying away thinking it has been deserted. It is advisable to use the same procedures as for introducing a cat to a new home – which this temporarily will be – and not allow it outside at first, nor then very far, until it has got used to the new location.

Right: Book boarding accommodation well in advance. Catteries get very busy at holiday times.

Residents of the United Kingdom, Australia, Eire and the State of Hawaii will only be able to take their cats on local holidays for they all have strict quarantine regulations to control the spread of rabies. Any cat entering these countries must spend time in carefully controlled quarantine conditions – six months in Britain – a great strain to put upon cats and owners. If you travel to or from these countries leave your cat behind unless you are moving permanently – or at least for a stay of such duration that it makes a separation of six months on your return seem worthwhile. Quarantine catteries have to be built and run to very stringent regulations and boarding in them is not cheap.

If you are away from home for any reason try to arrange for someone to stay in the house or come in to feed your cats and look after them. Most cats are more disturbed by a change of place than by people being away. They will usually cope well with someone else, especially if their regular schedule is maintained. Some, especially indoor cats, which are very attached to particular individuals, may be upset and perhaps go off their food but if they are given a little attention and played with at games they like they will not take it too badly – and some do not seem to mind at all. However, on your return, that does not mean that they will not put on a great demonstration of having been neglected! Older cats which are very set in their ways and have not been used to being boarded can be rather disturbed by going to a cattery so make every effort to have them looked after at home.

Some cats, especially if they get used to it when young and learn that it is only for a short time, adapt easily to a couple of weeks of being boarded in an ordinary cattery. They are kept separately from other cats (although cats used to living together can be housed together), they have a new world to look out on and a lot of new feline aquaintances to see and smell in neighbouring pens. Charges vary but are much lower than for quarantine boarding. Boarders must be inoculated (and have

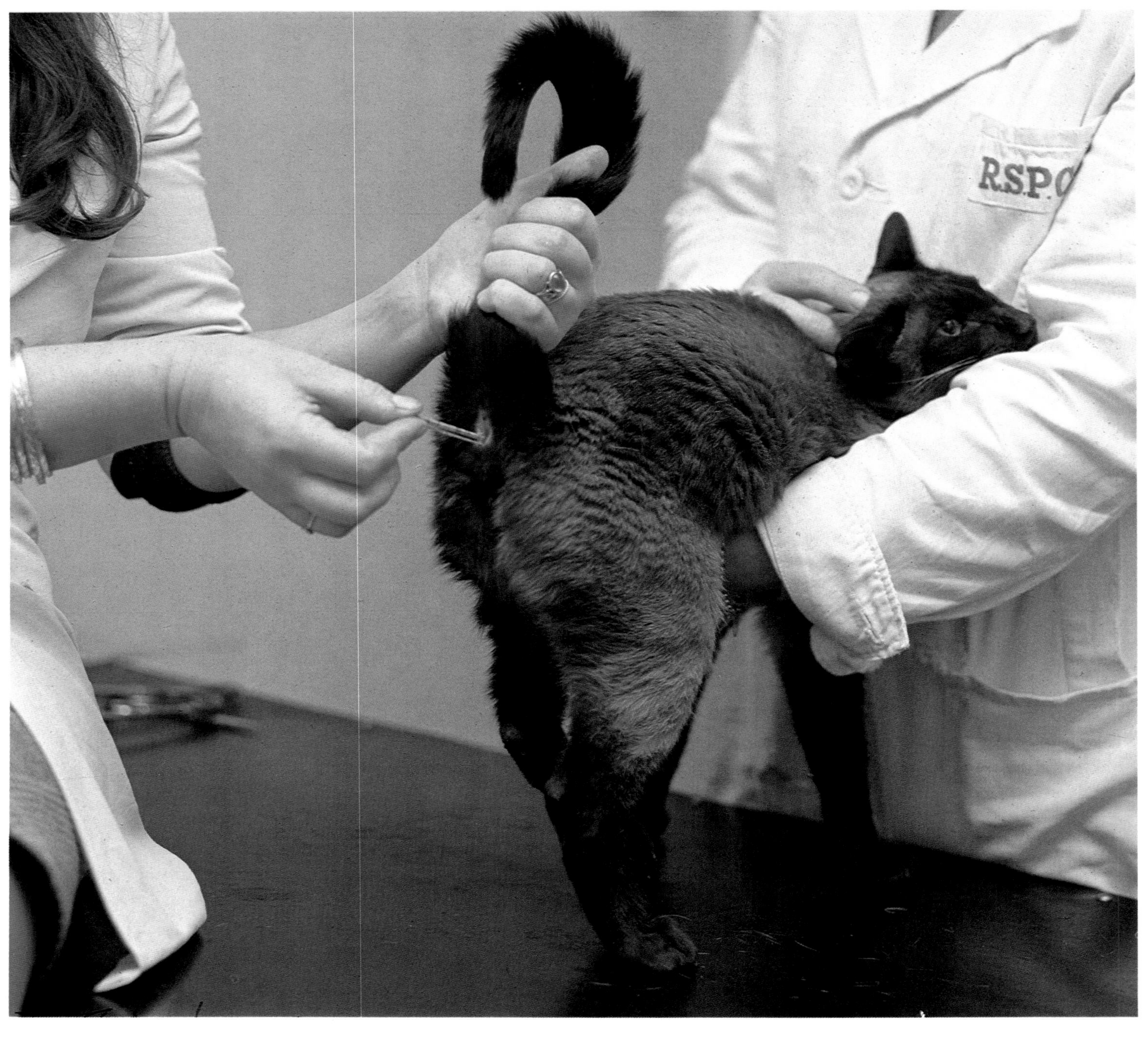

A cat's temperature is usually taken by inserting a thermometer in its rectum. The typical clinical thermometer used for humans is too fragile and a much stronger one is required.

certificates to prove it) and free of any parasites or infections, for other cats must not be put at risk. Good catteries have regular veterinary attendance and any problems which develop unexpectedly will be carefully dealt with, and some catteries are prepared to take on sick cats in certain circumstances. Unless a cat has to have a special diet for health or treatment reasons do not expect special food or attention to be given. Many faddy cats suddenly lose their faddiness when they are away from home! Assistants will not usually handle cats – any risk of spreading possible infection must be avoided – but may have time to remember a particular game or habit if you tell them. Some people like to leave a familiar piece of blanket or a toy with their pet. Many boarding catteries get booked up well in advance, especially for holiday times, so if you know you are going to be away plan well ahead. If you have trouble finding a good boarding cattery your vet or local animal welfare organization may be able to recommend one – you can always try the phone directory, though a personal recommendation is better. Check the place well in advance and find out what regulations the owners make.

Illness

Choosing a vet is up to you and your animals. Perhaps there is only one in the neighbourhood. If the breeder from whom you get your cat is local he or she will be able to advise – but, like choosing a doctor, it is a matter of finding someone with whom you and your animals can form a good relationship. Many practices are partnerships and you may find one of the practitioners more in sympathy with you than another. Certainly some vets have a greater understanding of cats than others. There are also animal welfare clinics which offer a full professional service to those who cannot afford to pay private fees – but they are frequently under pressure and should not be taken advantage of by those who can well afford private veterinary medicine, for which some insurance companies now offer policies.

Vets do not like people who waste their time, but they would rather see an animal that you are worried about and find nothing wrong with it than have you bring it in only when it is already very sick. Early diagnosis and treatment are always best. Try to report to the vet anything that you notice about the animal or its behaviour that differs from the normal, especially listlessness, lack of appetite, vomiting, diarrhoea, straining to pass urine; excessive scratching, washing or biting; lumps, wounds, dirt or powder in the fur, and so on. Listen carefully to any instructions the vet gives you for treatment – preferably write them down – and make sure that you really understand them. A vet will not mind repeating details or showing you once again how to carry out treatment or replace dressings if that will ensure that they are done correctly.

Most veterinary practices run an appointments system and if you telephone first to make an appointment you will save a great deal of waiting. Always take your cat to the vet in a travelling box or basket so that it cannot come into contact with other sick animals and will be easily controllable.

Panleukopenia, or **Feline Infectious Enteritis,** has already been mentioned as the most serious cat disease. Inoculations against it must be given as early as possible, from six weeks of age, and may be single shots or given in two doses. They will require booster shots from time to time throughout the animal's life. A cat with this killer disease will usually become exceptionally quiet with the first notice-

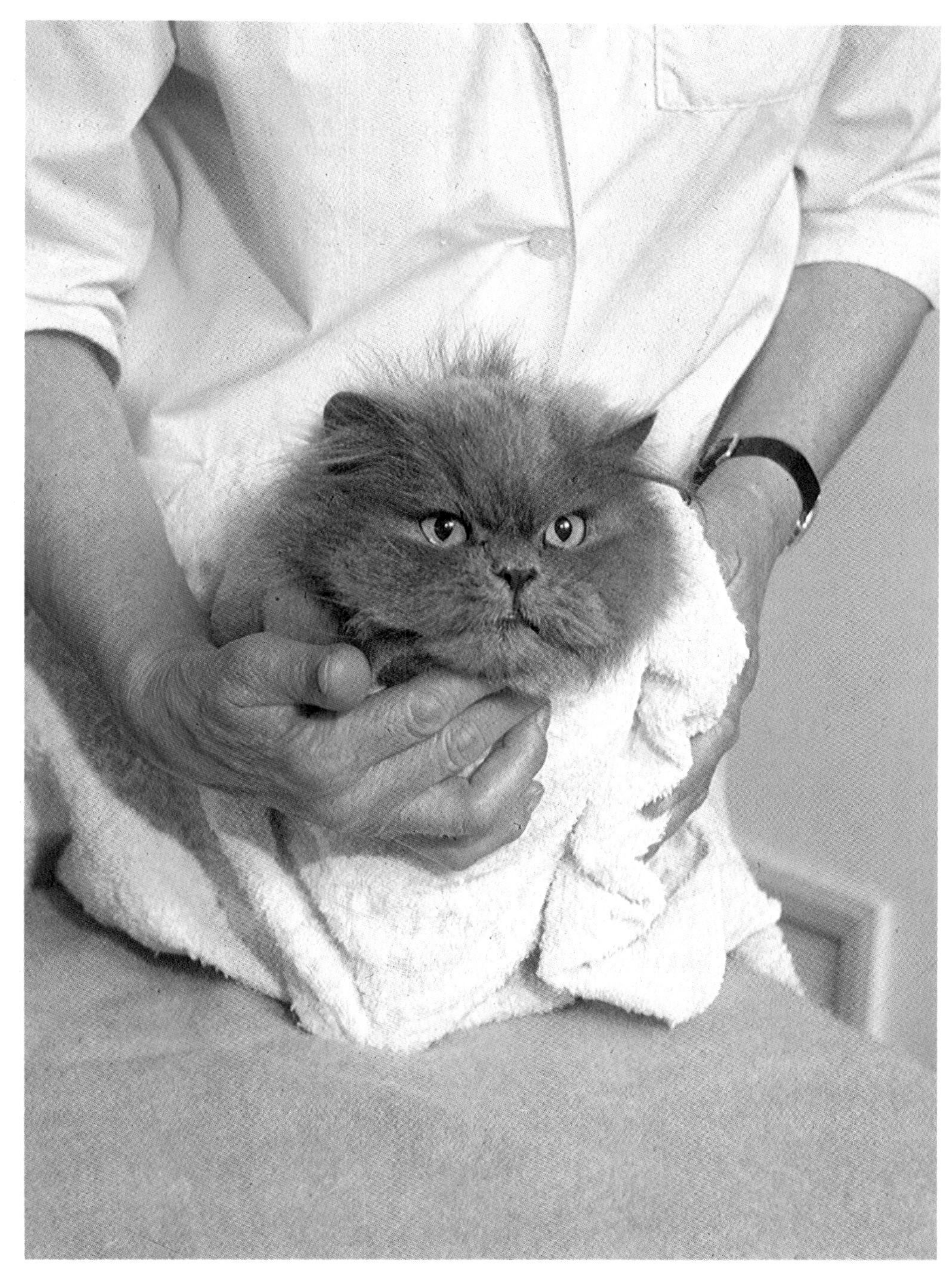

A towel will help restrain a nervous, struggling cat – but cats often seem to understand that the vet is only trying to help.

This sad litle four-week-old is a victim of cat 'flu.

able symptoms being vomiting (often prolonged and severe) producing froth and bile. Diarrhoea, high temperature and loss of appetite are usual and, although the cat becomes increasingly dehydrated, it rarely drinks – even though it may sit hunched up by its water bowl.

Similar symptoms also occur for **Feline viral rhino tracheitis** and **Feline piconravirus** infections – two diseases which are both commonly known as cat 'flu. There is usually sneezing, snuffling and dribbling from the mouth. If the cat is carefully nursed and holds out for more than a couple of days with these diseases it stands a good chance of pulling through but nonetheless they are very dangerous. Vaccine has been produced which will give some protection against both these viruses but its efficacy is not so widely proved as the panleukopenia vaccine and frequent boosters are necessary.

Rabies is fortunately almost excluded from Britain by quarantine regulations and does not frequently occur in North America, but it is transmissible to humans and some other animals and nearly always fatal to those who catch it and so must be taken very seriously if suspected. Rabies has two forms: furious rabies and dumb rabies. In the first the animal becomes very quiet and hides itself in dark corners. After a few days it may become very bad tempered and violent, savagely attacking everything that it meets with tooth and claw. Later it loses control of its muscles, becomes paralysed and dies. In dumb rabies the violent stage does not occur. Do not risk being bitten by a rabid cat (or dog) for the disease is transmitted in the animal's saliva. Lock it in if you can. Throw a cloth over it and try to place a box on top to trap it until veterinary or police help arrives and properly trained people can handle the situation.

Diseases such as cancer, peritonitis and leukaemia attack cats as they do humans but the most likely problems to occur will be parasites, and cuts and wounds sustained in fights or accidents. **Vomiting and diarrhoea** may mean a minor stomach upset which a day without food will probably put right but if they persist or are accompanied by other symptoms they must not be ignored. Pot bellies and scurvy skins are often signs of worms. Internal parasites may reveal their presence in vomit or in faeces. **Roundworms** are usually too small to notice, although they may be seen wriggling in any liquid brought up if you look carefully. **Tapeworms** are usually evident as small segments like long-grain rice in the fur around the cat's anus. Both are easily treated by pills if the infestation is caught early. **Ringworm** is not a worm at all but a fungal infection which produces raw patches on the skin. Under ultraviolet light most forms will show up as fluorescent rings. Ringworm is transmissible to humans and you should get your vet to treat it without delay. **Ear mites** appearing as black specks or, when bad infestation has been ignored, as an oily mess in the ear, can be treated with drops. **Fleas** are usually identified by scratching and black specks of excreta in the fur. Various powders and aerosols will deal with them, but since some flea killers are not suitable for cats it is always worth checking with your vet. Those which are pyrethrum based should be safe. Cat fleas are different from the human type and, although they may land on a human host and cause some irritation, they will not stay on you if there are cats around. Bedding, much-used furniture and room corners should also be treated with flea killer to kill off any remaining parasites or their eggs which may be lurking there. Eggs take about three weeks to turn into mature fleas so treat every ten days for a time to make sure that they do not survive and start up a new infestation. **Ticks** may be a problem in country areas. Oval-shaped and grey or brown in colour, they vary in size from a pinhead to a large seed. They attach themselves firmly to suck blood and may be so immobile they are mistaken for a cyst. They should be dabbed with alcohol or surgical spirit before being removed, or the mouth part will remain behind and cause a bad sore. **Lice** are not very common and are more likely to be found on kittens or sick cats. They should be treated in the same way as fleas.

Medication is usually given by injection or orally. Only in exceptional cases is a vet likely to suggest that you give injections. Subcutaneous injections (into the layer under the skin, usually given into the loose flesh on the scruff of the neck) can be administered by a careful person who understands what he or she is doing but intravenous injections require considerable skill – a cat's veins are smaller than those of a human being and more difficult to locate.

After treatment a cat's ears can be wiped clean with cotton wool, but cotton sticks should never be plunged deep into the ear.

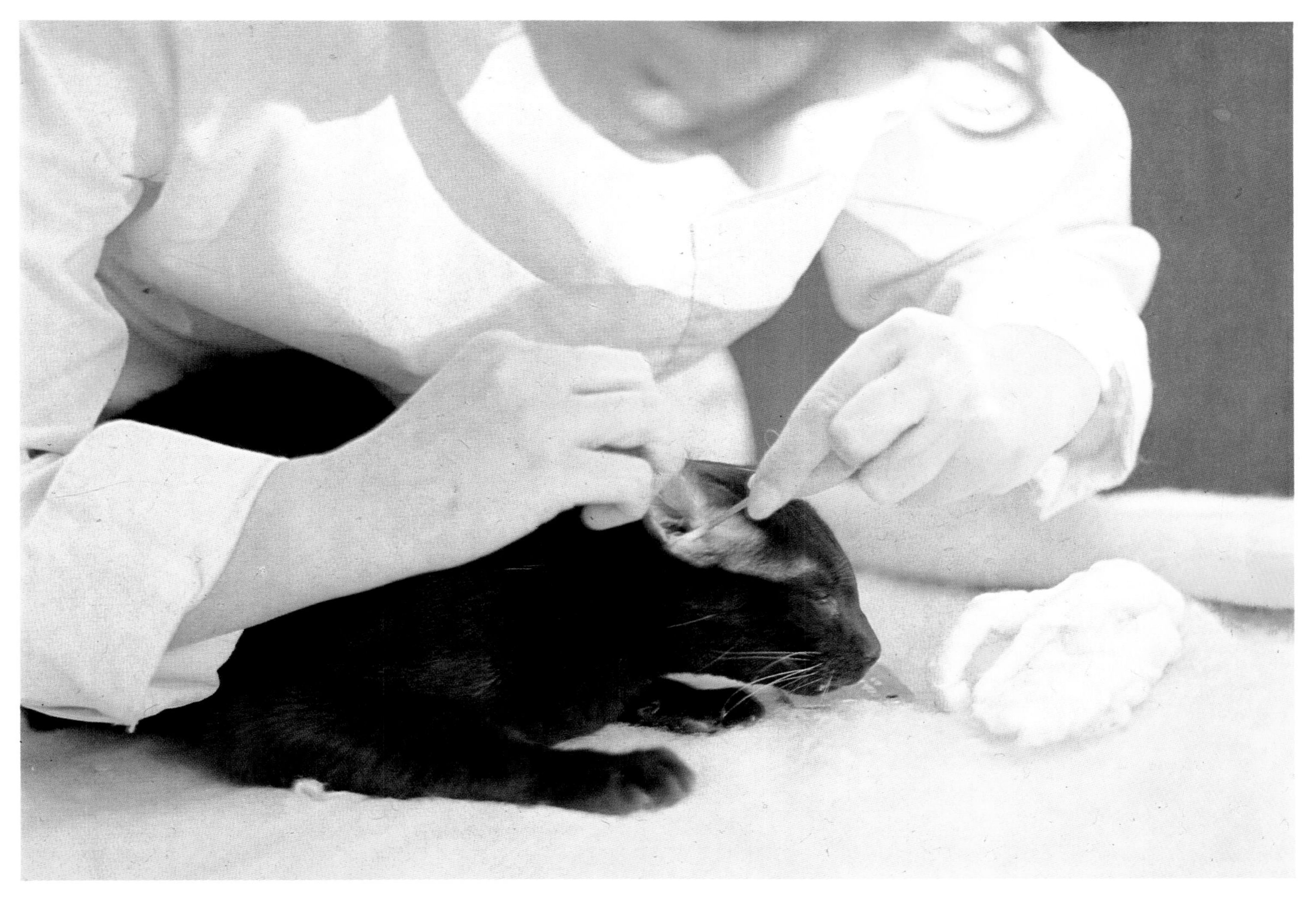

Some cats try to resist taking pills or, having accepted one, hold it in the mouth to spit out later. To make a cat open its mouth place one hand over the top of its head, squeezing gently at the sides of the mouth with the forefinger and thumb. Then put the pill on the back of the tongue with the other hand, hold the mouth closed and stroke the throat downwards until you are quite sure that the cat has swallowed. Do not let the cat go until it has opened its mouth again and confirmed that it has not just pretended to swallow. Some people prefer to hold the cat's mouth open with a spatula while they pop in the pill or use a special pill-giving device.

Liquid medicine is most easily given by syringe (without the hypodermic needle, of course) which enables a dose to be carefully measured and then squirted between the cat's teeth into the side of its mouth – a little at a time so that it does not choke the cat. A sick cat which refuses to eat or drink can be given water and liquid nourishment, such as meat essence, in the same way.

Cat's **scratches** and **surface wounds** usually heal rapidly. They can be bathed with a weak antiseptic solution (*not* carbolic).

Opposite: Wounds must be kept clean and germ-free – but remember never to use carbolic-based antiseptics with cats.

Below: Pressure on either side of the mouth will make a cat open it so that you can give a pill. Having someone else to restrain the cat will make it even easier.

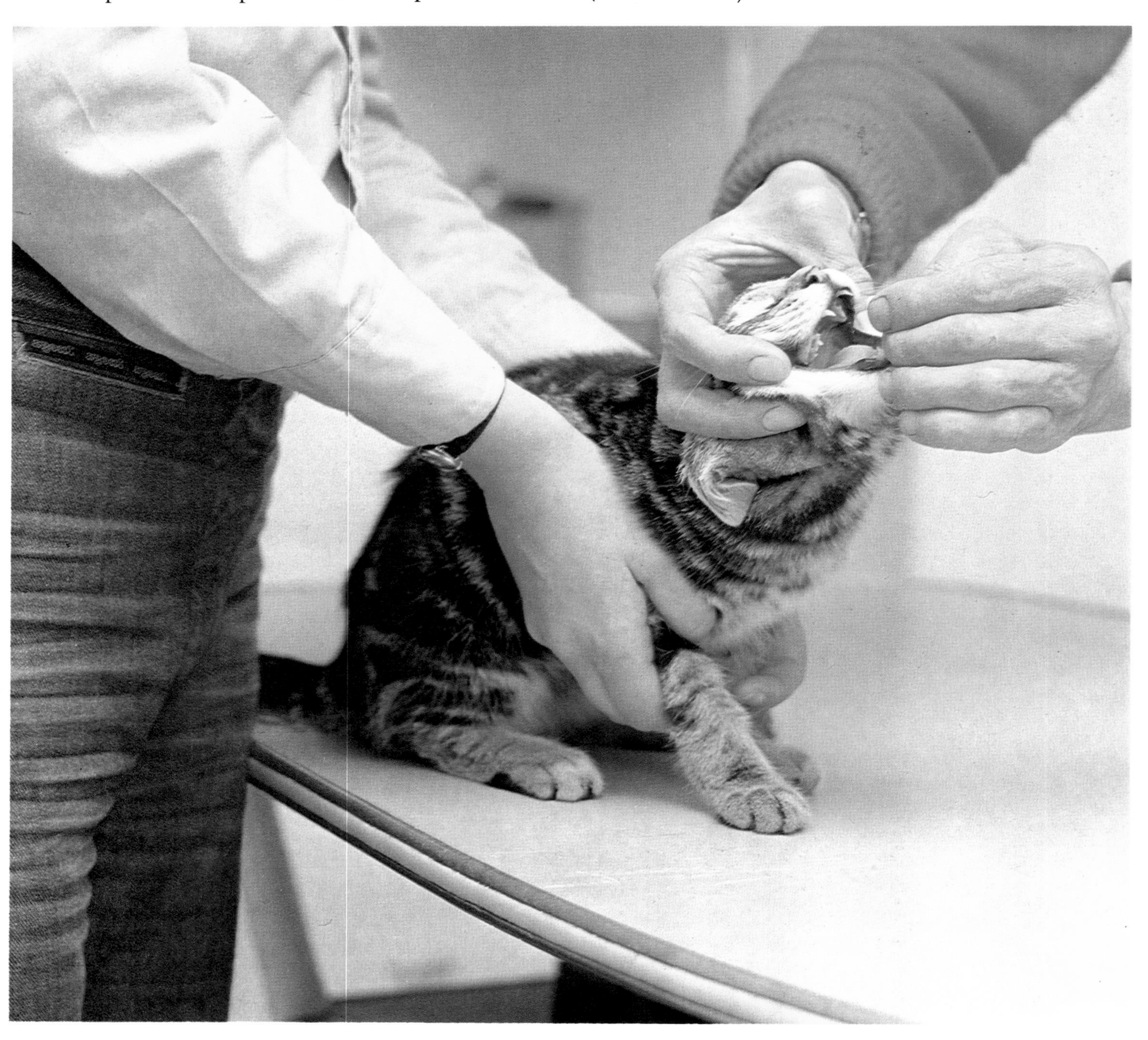

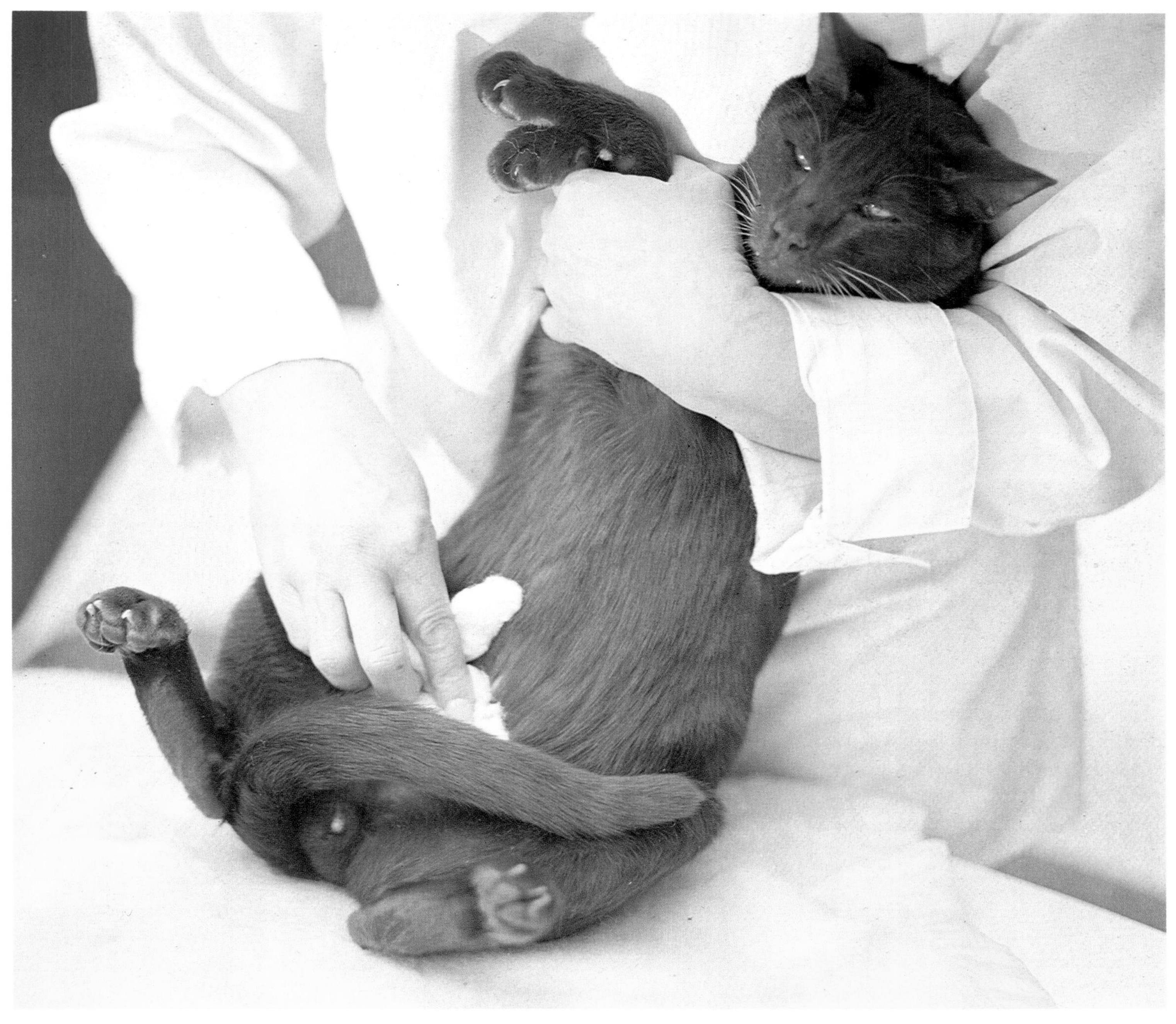

Sometimes this rapid healing encloses dirt or an infection and an abscess develops, an occurrence which is not uncommon following bites from other animals, but which will require professional attention.

Many disinfectants, weedkillers, paints, carbolic and petrol-based products are harmful to cats. Aspirin is particularly dangerous too and must never be given to them. If you have to keep poisons around the house or know that they are used in your neighbourhood (rat poisons, for instance) find out the appropriate antidotes and keep them to hand. If you think a cat has swallowed a poisonous substance telephone your vet and tell him what you suspect and any symptoms so that he can suggest an antidote if you do not have one. Your pharmacist can supply you with a 'universal mixture' which will be effective for many substances and you can keep some in your medicine chest. If you need to make an antidote in a hurry take one part of milk of magnesia, add two parts of powdered charcoal (burned toast will serve) and one of strong tea for a good formula. Hydrogen peroxide diluted in twelve times the amount of water is another instant emetic to make the cat vomit up the poison. If a cat has swallowed or tried to drink a caustic substance do *not* attempt to make it vomit. In all cases of poisoning get the cat to the vet as soon as possible.

If the cat gets a poisonous substance on its fur, wash it off with plenty of clean, cold water. Paint should not be removed with white spirit – it is better to cut away the fur. Paint on the paws can be removed with butter or lard.

Always handle a sick cat carefully. If it is frightened it may scratch or bite even people whom it normally trusts completely. Keep it warm and as quiet as possible on its way to the vet and let it have plenty of undisturbed rest when recuperating.

Opposite: *Longhairs, in particular, need regular grooming to keep their fur clean and free of tangles.*

Below: If a cat's claws need trimming it should be done with sharp clippers, not with scissors. Get your vet or an experienced owner to show you how.

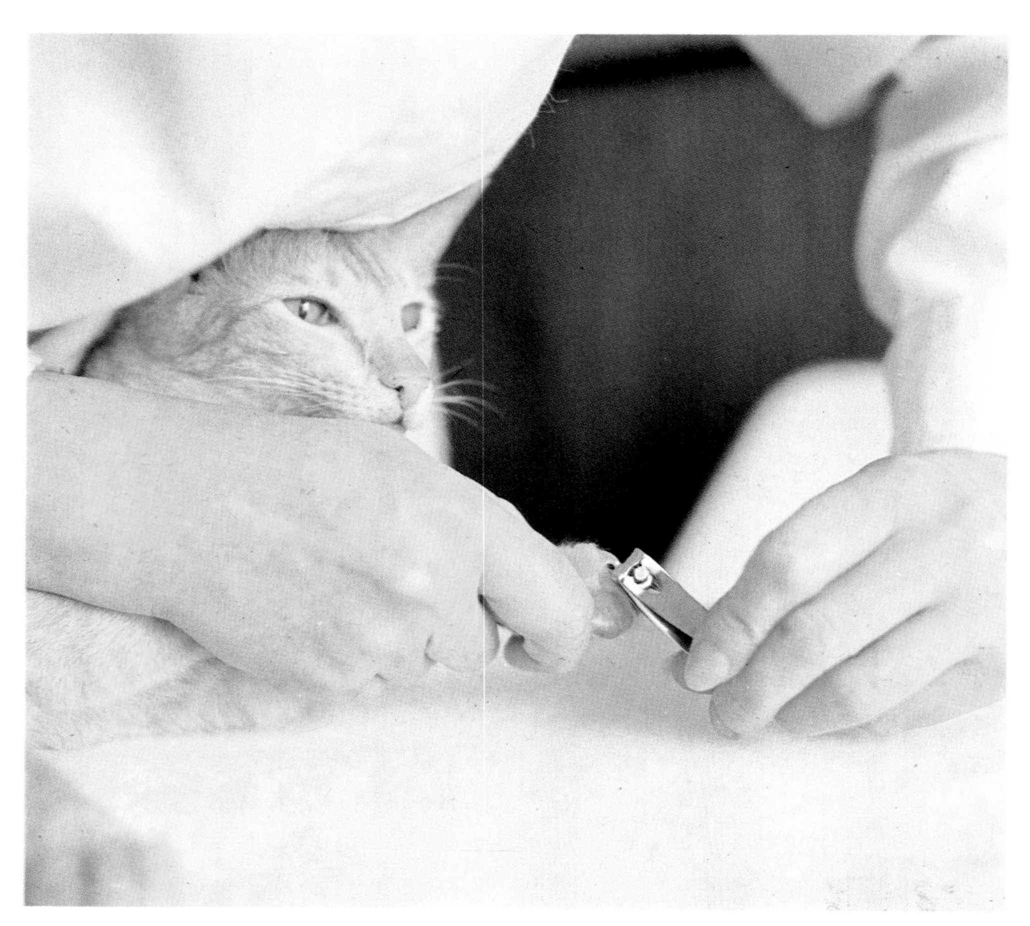

Grooming

Anyone who plays frequently with their cat and grooms it regularly will soon notice those small signs that show something is wrong. Grooming should include a check on mouth, eyes and paws as well as brushing and combing the fur. Longhaired cats should have their coats brushed at least once every day and a shorthair coat will also benefit from frequent attention. A brush with nylon bristles set in a rubber pad is suitable for longhairs and a baby brush for shorthairs. Do not use brushes with metal hairs, they can scratch the cat.

Brush vigorously in the same direction as the hair lies and against it. Longhairs should also be combed with a metal comb. One with very fine teeth will help to show fleas if their presence is suspected. Do not jerk at tangles and matts. Moistening often makes them easier to untangle but really bad matting may have to be cut away. Regular grooming will prevent it developing. When you have seen how much hair collects on the brush or comb you will understand why a cat which swallows it all produces hair balls – and why soft furnishings get covered with fur.

Start grooming by removing any burrs, then give a stimulating massage with the tips of the thumb and fingers, using plenty of pressure, in the same way that a barber gives a scalp massage. Cats seem to enjoy this and it helps to loosen dead hair. Then brush. Even hand grooming – firm stroking in effect – from head to tail will remove much of the moulted hair which will build up around the tail and can be easily picked off. To give an extra gloss to a short coat slip an old nylon stocking over the brush or use a piece of chiffon or a chamois leather to give a final grooming from head to tail.

If there is any dirt in the ears wipe them with a swab of cotton wool. Never poke anything into the ear. Remove any dirt from the corners of the eyes. Check the inside of the mouth and see that there is no tartar deposit on the teeth. A slight build up can usually be removed by scraping with a clean fingernail or smooth orange stick (if your cat lets you) but a hard encrustation will need descaling by the vet.

Check the paws and between the toes for any cuts or swellings. Cats which do not come into contact with hard surfaces to wear down their claws may need them trimming occasionally to prevent them becoming a nuisance to them or even curling back and puncturing the pad. Get a vet or other experienced person to show you exactly how to do this. Hold the paw and squeeze gently to make the cat extend its claws. Check them carefully in good light to see where the pink, live part of the claw ends. You must *not* cut near this. Use a pair of nail clippers, *not* scissors (the type that are spring-loaded and rather like secateurs are easiest to handle).

Another Generation

To observe the birth and rearing of kittens is a rewarding and fascinating experience but you should not allow your cat to have a litter unless you are prepared to look after them, and can guarantee good homes ready to take them. If you have a pedigree female and mate her with a suitable pedigree male you may be able to dispose of kittens without much trouble, indeed you will be able to charge something for them towards the cost of stud fees and rearing the litter. Mongrel kittens are not so easy to place, there are far too many of them about. Unless you have decided that you definitely are prepared to undertake the responsibilities involved you should have both male and female cats neutered. An adult female which can get out to encounter toms when she is in season will almost certainly become pregnant irrespective of your wishes.

Female cats are not prepared to mate at any time. Like most other mammals there are particular times when they will accept the attentions of a tom and are able to conceive. They are then known as being in season or on heat. Their bodies produce a special odour as a signal to male cats, and they also make a special call, which can be particularly loud and disturbing in orientals, sounding like a baby crying through the night. A female may stay on heat as little as three days if mated, or as long as a fortnight if not.

Some people can perceive the scent of the sex pheromone and the mating call is easily recognizable but there are other, earlier signs that a cat is coming on heat. She will become more affectionate, roll on the floor and wriggle ecstatically; she will probably purr and croon with pleasure if she is stroked or fondled and may raise her hindquarters, offering herself for copulation. Some females, kept in when in season, because their owners do not wish them to breed, seem to learn to suppress some of these signs, so that they are not prevented from going out to mate – but they cannot hide the queue of toms which lines up outside the house!

If you have a cat from which you wish to breed but for some reason want to prevent her mating for a time there is a drug, administered by injection or pill, which will prevent her from coming into season for six months. However, this drug changes a cat's hormonal balance and should not be used repeatedly. Some females are not eager to accept mating during their first season and many breeders feel it better to wait until a cat calls for the second time, especially with orientals, which mature sexually very early, so that she will be better able to raise a litter. However, doors and windows and any other possible exits must be kept shut and the calling cat closely watched so that she does not escape and mate with a marauding tom.

If you have a pedigree cat and want pedigree kittens find a breeder with a suitable stud tom well before you intend to breed. The breeder from whom you bought her will probably be able to suggest a cattery and perhaps advise on a tom with a suitable pedigree. Unless you are trying to produce a new variety you will usually mate like with like, but in some varieties this is not possible. Tortoiseshell and blue-cream cats are usually female and the few males are nearly always sterile so the females must be mated with a cat of one of their component colours. Manx are usually bred to tailed Manx because of inherent problems [see page 47]. Because certain types and colours have already been produced by mixing genetic stock great care must be taken to get the pairing right to produce the kittens that you want.

If cats with conflicting genes are mated certain characteristics will be dominant over others: for instance, black is dominant over blue and chocolate, short hair is dominant over long, all-over colour is dominant over Siamese points while a purebred black mated to purebred tabby will produce tabby. Even though these features may determine the appearance of a cat the other, recessive characteristic will still be carried and influence that cat's progeny; for instance, a mating between a Blue Point and a Chocolate Point Siamese does not produce either, the litter will all be

A female on heat may tread with her front paws, roll and twist on her back and raise her hindquarters.

Seal, the Siamese equivalent of black. A lilac occurs when parents carry recessive genes for both chocolate and blue.

Considerable research has been done on cat genetics and more information is still being assembled. For advice on breeding you should consult specialist books or expert breeders.

Having chosen the stud cat that you would like to use you wait for your female (called a queen) to come on heat. At the first signs of her season starting contact the tom's owner and check that he does not already have a female with him, or booked in, and reserve a space for when you both think will be the best time for mating: the third day of heat is generally considered the best for conception. You will pay a fee for the services of the tom and for the board of the queen while with him. Some breeders like the cats to spend several days together, others consider one is enough, provided that a mating has taken place.

Behaviour differs considerably according to the personalities of the cats. Many are very affectionate and seem to have a truly romantic liaison, others show no regard for the other animal. It is usual to let the cats get to know each other in adjoining pens before allowing them to approach each other.

When they are together the queen will usually reject the tom at first, although not always when both are gentle cats. The male will circle the female, talking to her and trying to sniff her hindquarters. She will probably spit at him and perhaps even strike out with a paw if he comes too close. When not keeping him away she will roll on the ground, crouch, making treading motions on the spot, and call back at him. Eventually she will allow him to approach and will

Right: The tom will stand over the queen, often gripping the scruff of her neck in his teeth, before beginning to tread up and down upon her with his paws.

Above: As the embryos develop within the mother their weight will slow her down and force her to be a little less active.

crouch with her head down and her hindquarters raised, her tail to one side. The tom will often take the loose skin on the back of her neck in his teeth as he stands with first his forelegs, and then all four feet, upon her. He treads up and down on her with his hind legs, gradually moving them backwards, and the female may be treading too. Then the tom begins to lunge forward. His hind legs return to the ground and the queen moves to balance his action and to present her vulva to him and enable him to insert his penis. This is not a straightforward procedure and many queens get impatient and irritated and break away from the tom so that the whole business has to start again – sometimes several times.

Ejaculation is extremely rapid, once intromission does take place, and is all over in a matter of seconds. On withdrawal the female usually makes a loud cry and sometimes turns on the tom. The adult tom's penis is covered with short barb-like spines and these may hurt the female as it is removed. After copulation the queen rolls around on her back, a movement which is thought to aid fertilization.

Most breeders like to witness more than one mating to be fairly sure that conception will take place. They will usually let the queen stay until these have occurred. When you collect your cat make sure that you have a copy of the stud cat's pedigree so that the kittens can be properly registered. Keep the queen away from other toms until she is completely off heat, or if she mates with another cat you may find that she will conceive by him, too.

Gestation in the cat takes sixty-three to sixty-five days. As in all mothers a birth can sometimes be premature, and a cat particularly close to its owner may occasionally delay giving birth if he or she is away from home. Siamese, in particular, may be overdue. A check-up at the vet's a week or so before the kittens are expected is always wise.

Your vet will be able to tell if the cat is pregnant after about three weeks. A reddening of the nipples occurs first and about a fortnight later they begin to swell. Sometimes an expert can even feel the embryos developing but trying to do so yourself may cause damage. You do not need to give her any special attention at first but do give her extra food when she begins to ask for it. She should also have extra vitamins and minerals, which you can get in powder form to mix with her food, but do not give too much or overfeed, for large kittens are more difficult to deliver. Continue these supplements after the kittens are born for as long as she is feeding them. Your vet will advise you on the quantities to suit your cat.

As the time for parturition approaches the queen will probably attempt to make a nest ready for the birth. Prepare one for her. A large cardboard box about 60 cm (2 ft) on all sides will serve. It should be lined with newspaper with a lid on top to keep out draughts and a hole cut on one side low enough for her to get in and out easily. Put it in a warm, dark corner where she can be quiet and undisturbed by household comings and goings and where you can keep other animals and children away from her. Place her in it occasionally and she may begin to tear up the paper in the box. If she does not want to adopt it note where she seems to prefer and move the box there if it is not impracticable. By making a positive nest for her you will avoid the possibility of her sneaking off to some dark inaccessible corner

A cat with a number of kittens may readily accept an orphan, like this white one, if it is made to smell like her own.

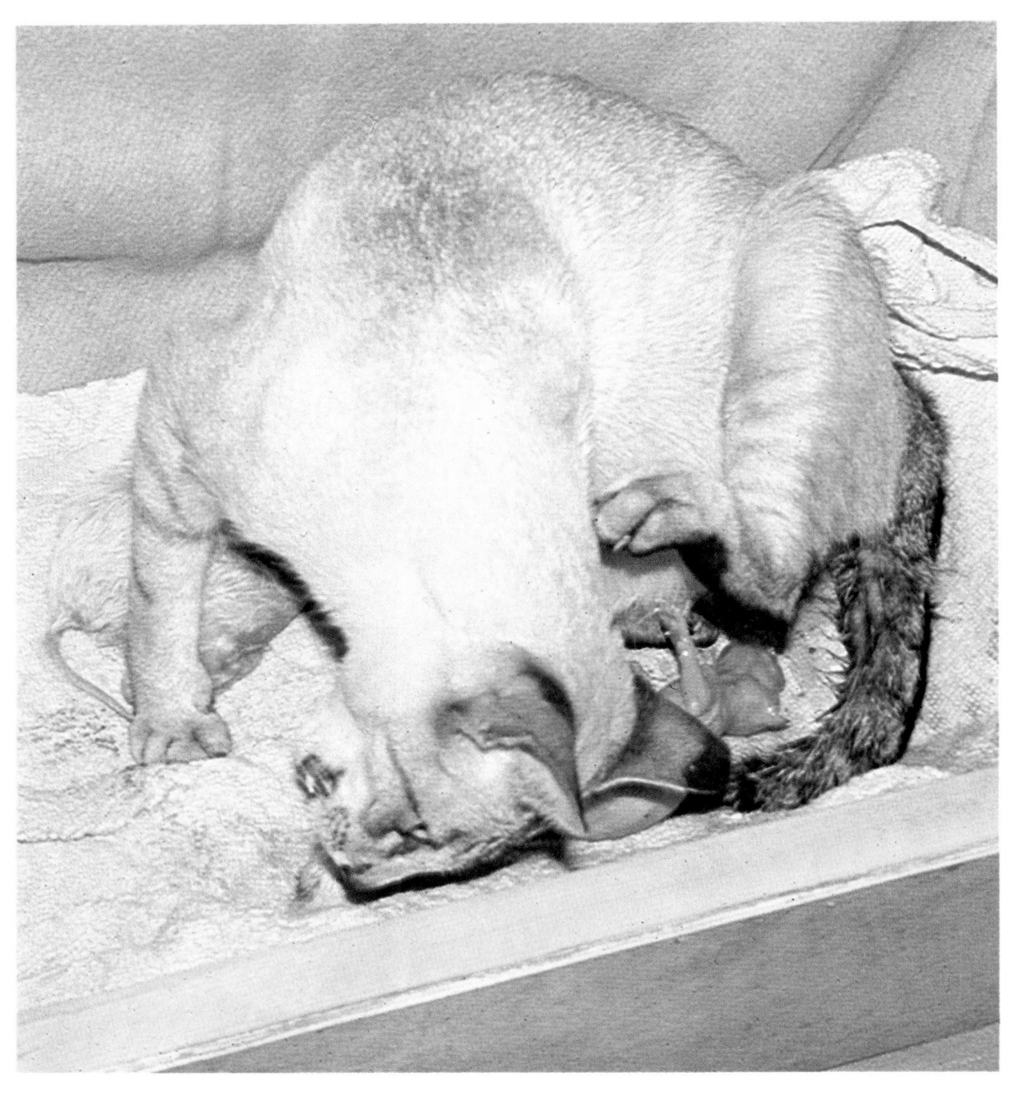

The moment of birth: the membrane, drawn tightly across the kitten's face, is already beginning to tear. The mother licks off the membrane and bites through the umbilical cord, then the new-born kittens are licked clean and dry. Four born – how many more to go? Time for a brief rest for mother. Meanwhile the first-born, already dry and fluffy-furred, is fighting for a nipple.

underneath furniture or in the bottom of a cupboard where you will not be able to help her in case of difficulties – and perhaps dissuade her from deciding to take over your bed.

Birth difficulties in cats are comparatively rare. Most queens take everything in their stride but some prefer human company and you should be ready to help if necessary. Some welcome the support of a sister cat, or even a male, but if they are not welcome make sure that other animals do not bother her or the kittens.

Signs that birth is imminent are usually increasingly affectionate behaviour, traces of milk on the nipples and perhaps a slight discharge of fluid from the vagina. A considerable discharge could mean something wrong and you should call the vet. The mother will almost certainly begin to behave rather erratically. Add a blanket to the kittening box – and a piece of towelling on top to keep it clean.

By this time you should not be letting the cat go outdoors, for she will not be able to cope with getting about or eluding attack as easily as she becomes more awkward with the burden of the kittens. Establish a litter tray in the room where you have made her nest. Even a cat used to going outside, if trained as a kitten to use litter, will usually rapidly adapt back to it. Transfer her food and water bowls to the same room, too.

Sometimes a queen may vomit from excitement, or because she has eaten too much, she will probably squat on her litter tray then suddenly give up and scratch, she may tear her bedding to shreds or rearrange it. Later she will probably begin to pant and may make crying noises. All these are signs of the first stage of labour. Some cats will fetch their owner to be present for the birth, others prefer to simply disappear and quietly get on with it.

The second stage of labour begins with straining – the cat is contracting her muscles to push the kittens out into the world. Her vaginal opening will have enlarged and be moist with lubricating liquid. After straining for a moment or two she will probably relax, then strain again. It may take only a few minutes for the first kitten to be delivered, but frequently it takes half an hour and there is little you can do to help. Usually the kitten will still be in its sac, shrouded in membrane, which sometimes has already been torn open. In either case it will still be attached by the umbilical cord to the placenta, still inside the mother. She immediately starts licking the kitten, removing and usually swallowing the membrane, and

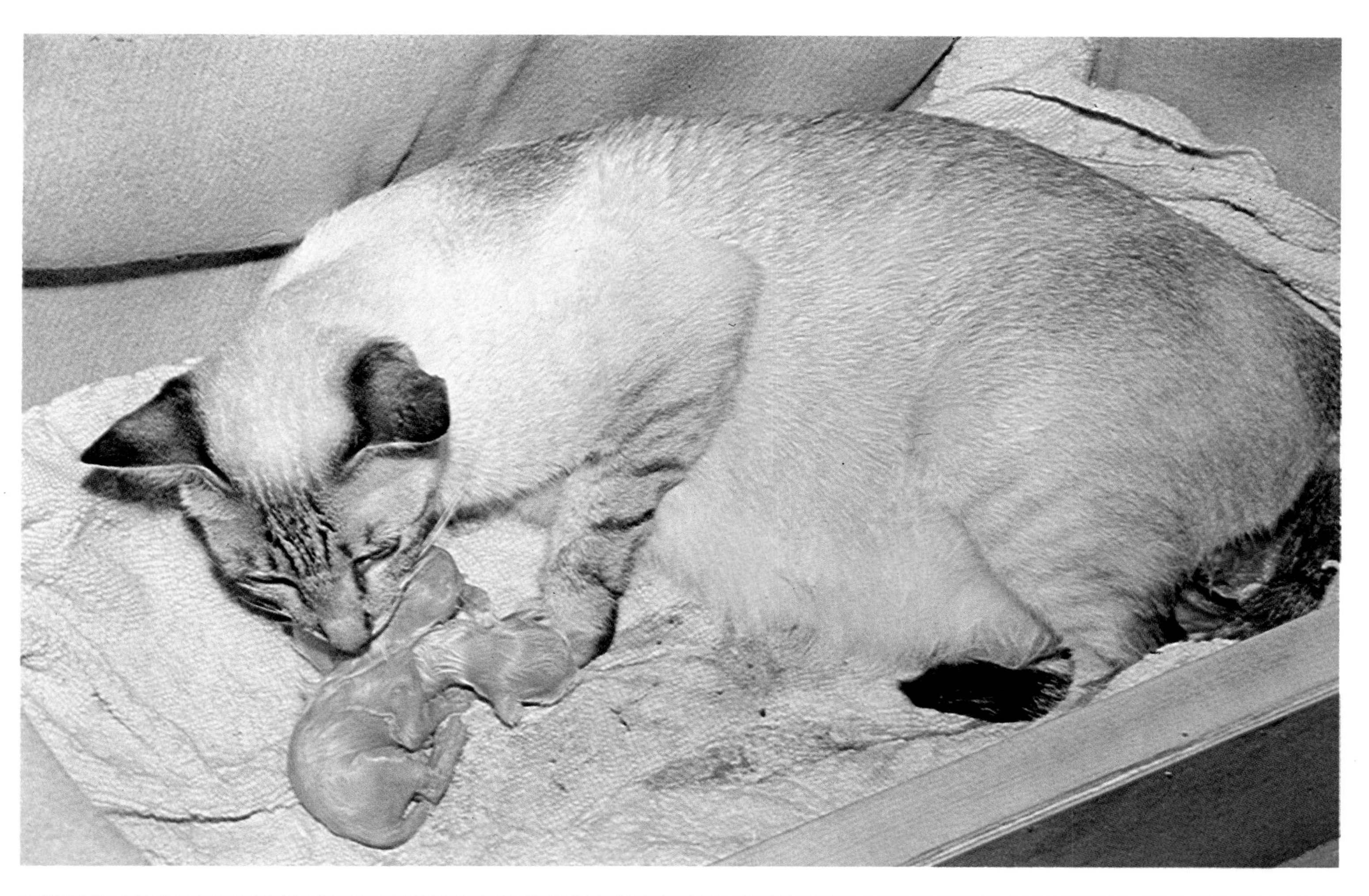

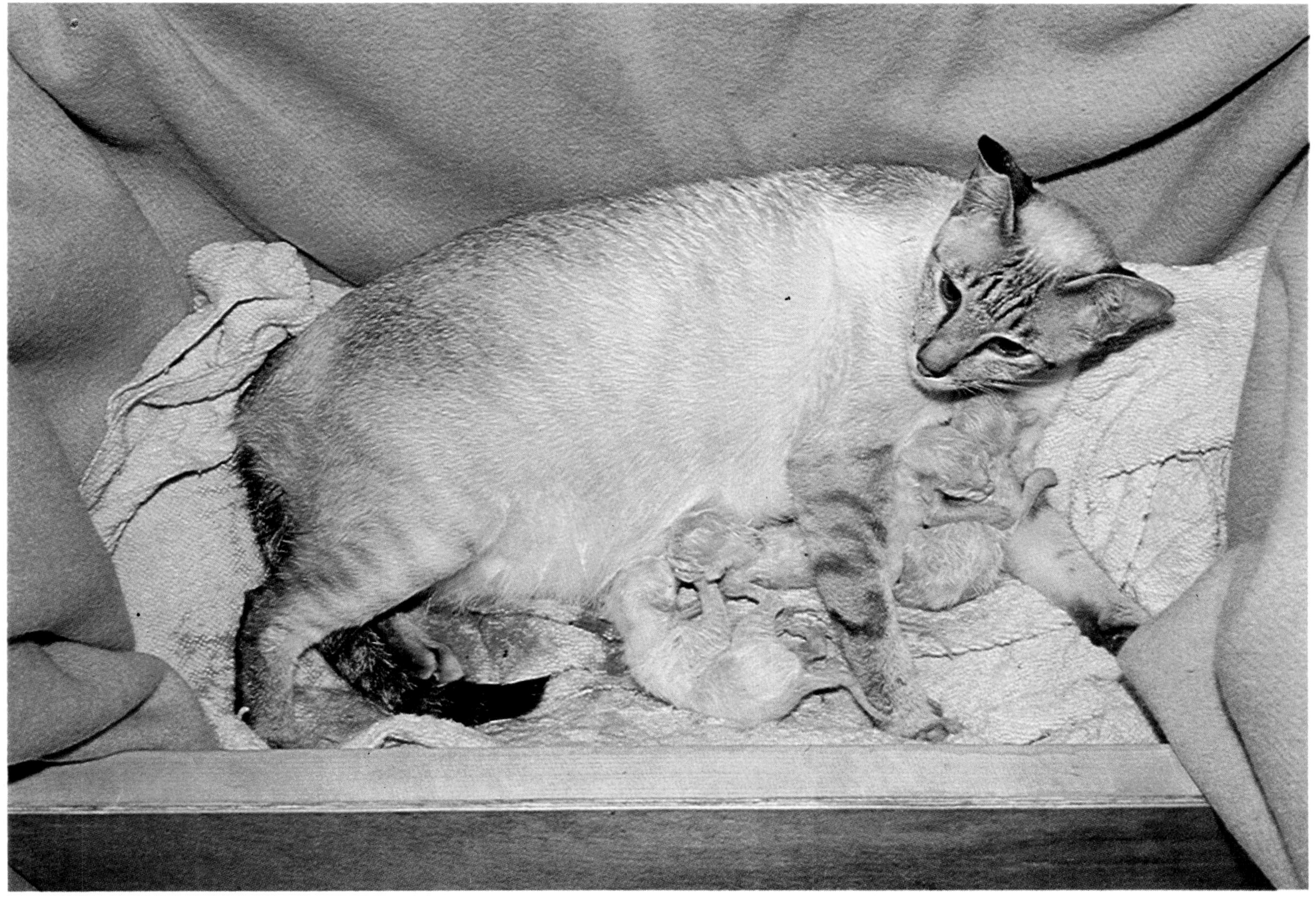

severing the umbilical cord. The kitten begins to gasp until it is actually breathing rhythmically. It may even start to squeak and soon it will move in the direction of its mother's nipples. Then the mother expels the placenta and will usually eat it, too. Then there is a respite before the contractions begin for the birth of the next kitten – usually a gap of from five to fifteen minutes. After the second kitten, the later ones tend to be born closer together. Sometimes kittens come in rapid succession and their mother has no time to do more than break the membrane to clear their heads – cleaning up has to wait until later.

Occasionally inexperience in the mother or the speed of delivery make it necessary to help with freeing the kitten's head to enable it to breathe, and to sever the umbilical cord. Your hands should be clean and sterilized in Dettol or a similar safe antiseptic. You can tear open the sac with your fingers and clean the kitten with a piece of rough towel, make sure that its mouth is clear of mucus and rub its body vigorously to start it breathing. To sever the umbilical cord grip it near the kitten's body between the fingers and thumb of one hand and, about 3 in (8 cm) away, grip it in the other between the thumb and index finger, rubbing them to and fro until it separates. A hot-water bottle wrapped in a towel will keep the kittens warm until their mother is able to accept them. As a desperate measure, if a kitten appears dead, it is sometimes possible to start it breathing by grasping both its rear legs and, keeping both arms straight and together, swinging it up and down in an arc – but this is a risky technique for the untrained and is a last resort.

Usually a kitten is born head and forelegs first and if a cat seems to give up halfway through a delivery you may be able to draw the kitten out by wrapping a sterilized piece of towel around the protruding

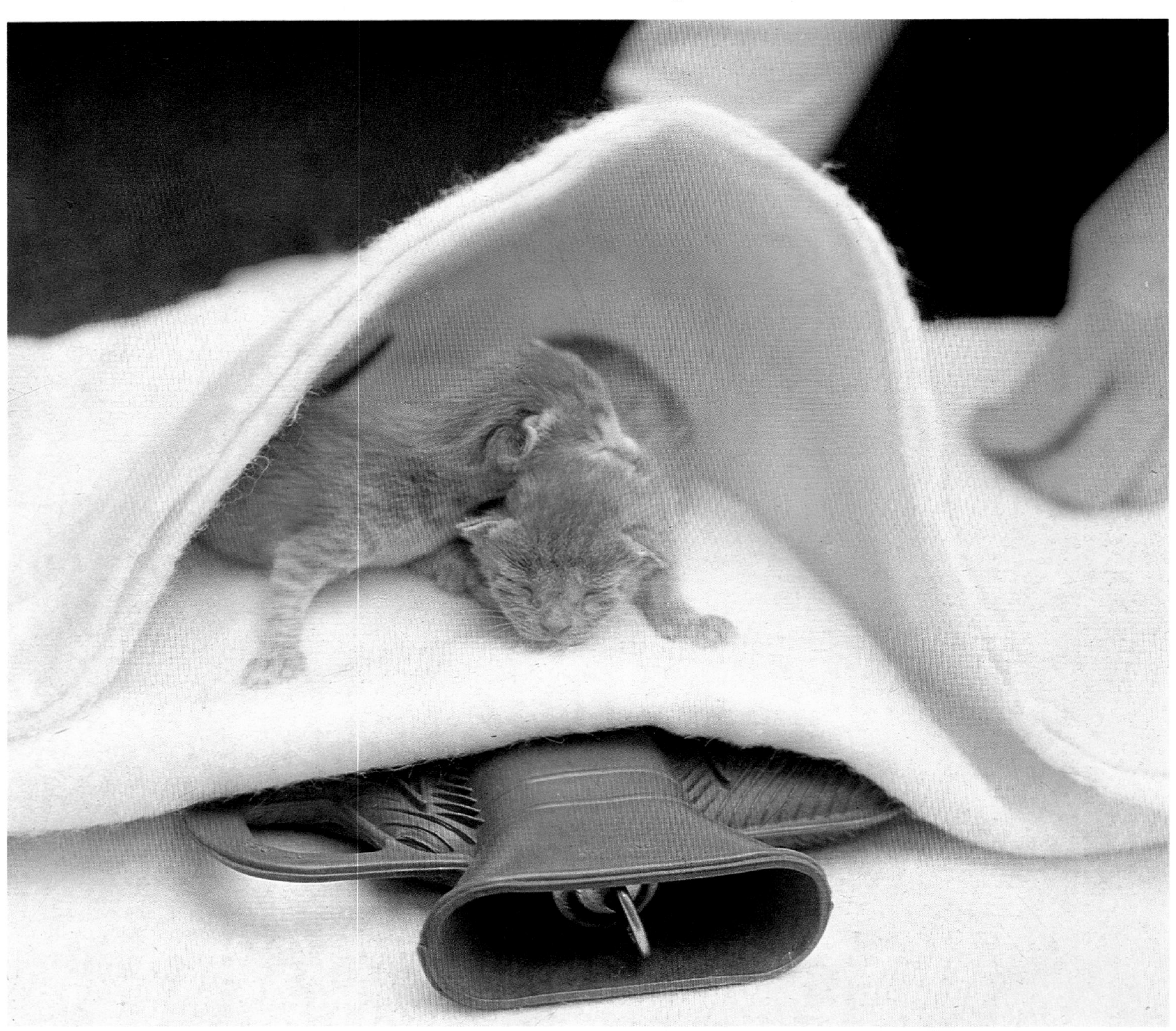

Opposite, below: A hot-water bottle and a blanket will do a fine job in keeping kittens warm.

Right: Sexing kittens: male right, female left.

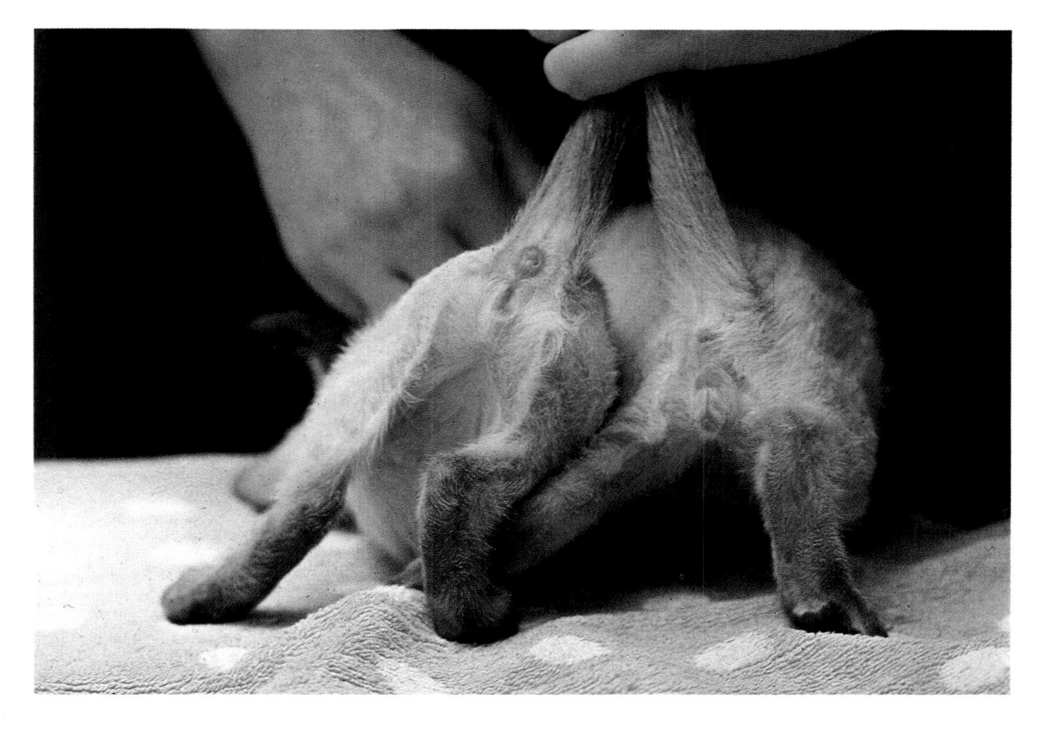

A Chocolate Siamese and her kittens. Siamese kittens are born without their colour points which develop as they grow.

part and gently easing it out – it usually helps to push it slightly back in first and then pull gently with a side-to-side motion. Do not tug on its legs or you may tear the kitten in two – and always check that the protruding limbs come from the same end of the body. If they do not and you have a breech birth get the vet, or rush the cat to him as quickly as you can. If that is impossible at least get the vet on the telephone, explain the situation and act on his instructions.

If kittens do not make their way to their mother's belly, guide them in the right direction. Never let them wander away from her, for if they are exposed to cold or draughts they may die very quickly.

In all births that you observe make sure that the mother also delivers a placenta (or afterbirth), for each kitten, for should one be retained inside her body it may decay within her. She would then probably go off her food and produce a brown discharge from her vagina, symptoms which show up two or three days after delivering the litter. At that stage she can easily be treated by your vet – but ignored the condition can be dangerous.

Sometimes a cat may go for a drink or even eat during delivery of the litter, and sometimes the mother behaves as though all the kittens have arrived, and settles down to looking after them, although she is still carrying kittens, and there may be a gap of as much as twenty-four hours before the remainder of the litter is born.

Litters are usually from four to six in number but can range from a single kitten to as many as a dozen. Few cats can be expected to rear more than six without some difficulty and your vet should be consulted as to how many it would be wise to leave with her. Hand-rearing kittens is difficult and it is often wisest to have the weaker surplus kittens removed as soon as possible and humanely killed, or it may be possible to hand-feed the kittens in rotation so that they do not make such heavy demands on their mother. Special formula powdered milk is made for rearing kittens and is much better than trying to mix up your own substitute. Trying to raise orphan kittens or kittens which a mother has rejected requires great patience and should be done under veterinary advice.

When kittens are born their eyes are closed and they use their sense of smell to find their mother's nipples and to find their way over short distances away from the nest.

Right: All kittens are born with blue eyes which later change to the adult colour for the breed.

Below: Farmyard mouser or pure-bred pedigree, most cats make dutiful and caring mothers.

Usually each kitten claims a particular nipple, which reduces squabbles at feeding-time if there are enough to go around. Sometimes the lowest nipples on the body provide little milk and the kittens left with these nipples may need supplementary feeding. Most litters grow and gain weight rapidly. You will easily be able to see if one kitten is falling behind. If the whole litter fails to gain weight check that the mother is not building up surplus milk. There is a little-understood condition known as the 'fading kitten syndrome' in which they stop suckling and consequently rapidly fade and die. Forcible hand-feeding rarely succeeds in saving the kittens and the build-up of milk can also be dangerous for the mother.

The kittens' eyes – which at first are always blue – open after about eight days but they do not properly use their sight until they are two or three weeks old. By this time they may begin to sample their mother's food and you can try offering them some evaporated milk or formula powdered milk. If they successfully 'lap it up try mixing in a very small quantity of cooked cereal – canned baby foods are quite suitable. They will now be suckling when they wish, provided that their mother allows it, and she will be showing them a little less attention. Gradually they will take more food and rely less on her milk. Should any not be learning to lap, offer them milk on a clean fingertip, or dab a little on their noses to make them lick.

When the kittens begin to get their milk teeth, usually from about four weeks old, you can start giving them some very finely-chopped or minced meat and some lightly scrambled egg until they

A mother cat keeps her kittens clean, massaging their stomachs to stimulate digestion and licking them to encourage evacuation.

Something is threatening her kittens, so this mother is patiently carrying them, one by one, to a place of safety.

are having five or six small meals a day and going to their mother only for a bedtime snack. If they still demand to be fed by her and are not being naturally weaned you must keep them apart from her or the situation could go on indefinitely and be very exhausting for her. Fresh drinking water should be available for mother and kittens all the time. Diet for the growing kitten is given on page 87.

Most female cats make excellent mothers – and some males make good nurses too. In the first fortnight of their lives a queen will be constantly caring for her kittens, nuzzling them awake and encouraging them to suckle, licking their bellies from top to bottom to stimulate digestion and keeping their orifices clean. When they stray she will summon them with a gentle high-pitched call or even go out and drag them back by the scruff of the neck. If she feels danger threatens she may pick up the whole litter, one by one, and carry them to somewhere she considers more secure. She will lie twitching her tail for them to play with and encourage them to pounce and chase, pretending not to notice until the last moment of their attack. She may bring still-living prey back to them to show them how to kill.

From about the fifth week on kittens will instinctively follow their mother for quite long distances, and, as explained on page 124, this following reflex can be transferred to people. If the mother hunts they will learn how to catch prey.

The mother will gradually spend less time with the litter, and thus increase their independence. Playing with each other they can practise the skills of camouflage, ambush, stalking, attack and defence that they will need for adult

life. Despite the violent rough and tumble, injuries are extremely rare and very minor. There seems to be an instinctive restraint from any harm being done, a restraint which the tension of a real fight removes. Often a game will suddenly stop and the chaser and chased change roles. A fluttering leaf becomes make-believe prey – and seems much less intimidating than a spider, for kittens seem very wary of the slower-moving creatures until they learn that a spider or a fly can be a quite delicious titbit.

It is at this lively kitten state that cats are perhaps their most obviously delightful, as all young creatures tend to be. Making pets of animals seems to extend that kitten stage for, not needing to devote their lives to the quest for food and self-preservation, cats can go on playing the games of youth. It is by encouraging these games, by being a surrogate mother in caring for and playing with your cat, that you will keep it young at heart and a delight to own for the whole of its life.

Mother cats are extremely tolerant with their kittens, but leave no doubt as to who is in charge.

Understanding Your Cat

Cats are not pack animals but solitary creatures, except at mating times, and when juvenile the wild cat lives alone. The development of colonies of semi-feral cats in some big cities may seem a contradiction, but there is no evidence that the individual animals in the colony hunt together (as do lions, for instance), and they are probably as protective of their restricted territories as penguins on an Antarctic shore. Nevertheless, the hunting ranges of feral cats often overlap where several animals may use the same route and there appear to be places where cats may deliberately meet, not just for mating but for an apparently social gathering, usually at night.

A dominance hierarchy seems to develop in any particular neighbourhood but may not be rigidly enforced. A dominant cat perhaps will tolerate an inferior, waiting until it has cleared a communal route or vacated a favourite sunbathing spot, rather than risk a confrontation which could challenge its dominance. Urban cats, in particular, must accept much greater proximity than cats in the countryside.

The domestic pet is in an artificial situation. An indoor cat, sharing its home with humans and with other animals, will be excluded by the humans from certain parts of the home and may only be able to establish claims to very restricted places – a basket, a chair – and then perhaps only for a short time, after which another cat may be permitted to share or even to take over

This tabby shows a mixture of interest and apprehension, while the tortoiseshell and white appears to be pulling back a little, its head slightly lowered and ears partly flattened in a submissive gesture.

the place. This is particularly true when cats are allowed to sleep on their owner's bed – one claims precedence for a few minutes, the other curling up alongside once that precedence has been demonstrated.

To a certain extent a pet animal is living in an artificially extended juvenile state. Some dog breeds appear to be genetically more infantile than others, remaining perpetual puppies in their emtional development. Cats have not been domesticated for so long and remain much more independent but human interference does affect their behaviour. A kitten taken from its mother and litter mates too young may not have had enough social interaction with other cats and may grow up aggressive towards them, leading to problems in accepting a mate and rearing kittens and to an over-dependence upon humans. Insufficient play with other kittens may prevent it from learning when to sheathe its claws to avoid inflicting injury. Mother cats often bring live prey back to their litter and a kitten without this experience may never associate prey with food or learn the correct way to kill.

A kitten which stays long enough with its siblings and also

Left: Washing each other, especially those places awkward to reach with one's own paw and tongue, is a friendly gesture among cats.

has plenty of attention from its owner will have the advantage of continual stimulus to make it lively and develop its intelligence. Early handling by humans will help to give it confidence in people, especially if more than one person is involved, and holding it will get it used to being restrained. Stroking and handling after the manner of its mother perhaps extends the juvenile emotional responses into adult life, although the animal becomes physically mature. Certainly many cats show aspects of infantile behaviour in later life, as well as maintaining the liveliness of kittenhood. Purring may be an instance. Why cats purr is not very clear. It may be a signal from a kitten to its mother to let down milk, on the other hand most mothers themselves purr almost continuously while nursing. Perhaps the kitten simply learns to associate it with pleasure, the pleasure of being fed. Kittens also push their paws around the nipple, to encourage milk to flow, and dribble in anticipation. Many cats continue to produce these actions involuntarily when they are being cuddled, or even suck on a jersey or other piece of clothing when in this super-happy state.

A cat's mood is usually clearly indicated by its behaviour. A happy cat will hold its tail boldly in

Below: Two's company – and cosy too!

This cat is approaching with confidence, its tail held high and slightly curling at the tip.

the air, especially when it runs to greet you. This too seems to be an infantile survival. It is the way a kitten approaches its mother and may be derived from the mother's cleaning of its anogenital area. When cats greet each other like this one often sniffs the hindquarters of the other, or even licks them, as a mother cat would do. On meeting, two cats will often sniff the areas of their major scent glands and, if very friendly, rub their noses or heads against each other.

Tail, ear, head and body positions, pupil dilation and the erection of the fur are all expressive of a cat's feelings. A confident cat issuing a warning to another will bring its ears forward, slightly lower its head and raise its hindquarters, staring at the object of its attention. A submissive cat may first turn its head away and lick itself. This 'displacement activity' is frequent in the cat, which will wash itself to hide any embarrassment, such as being seen failing to catch a fly, or when it cannot decide what to do – 'when in doubt, wash' seems to be a feline proverb. The next stage will be to bow its head, lowering its ears and crouching, making itself as small as possible. Frequently a cat will present a combination of the two reactions, in situations where it feels threatened and warns the offender to go no further. The rear is raised and advances, the tail often held high with all the fur standing on end, like a bushy Christmas tree, while the head is lowered and the front part of the cat retreats, pushing the back into an arch which makes the animal look bigger and more threatening, especially if it turns slightly sideways to its aggressor. As the cat increases its threat its pupils dilate, its ears become flatter, providing less of a target (ear injury in fights is quite common), more and more of the body hair becomes erect and the cat may display its teeth, growling and spitting.

Vocal communication in the cat can be extensive and some will carry on considerable 'conversations' with humans – Siamese can be particularly chatty. Some owners claim to understand exactly what their cat is saying and that their cat can understand them. In any cat and human interaction some mutually comprehensible signals will be understood and the extent of communication will probably be related to the closeness of the relationship. There may be features exclusive to an individual or a household which have developed to have their own meanings, but some sounds appear to be common to most cats.

Apart from the purr, which usually indicates contentment, although some cats produce a deep purr when in pain or real distress, there are the chirrupy sounds which a mother cat makes to her kittens and the comforting crooning with which she reassures them. A more plaintive croon is used by the courting males and a similar soft call used to humans becomes a polite please, rising in intensity to a harsh demand or a howl of complaint. There is the sharp cry of pain and the oestral call of the female, the scream of anger and the caterwauling song with which some cats beguile the night. There is a strange, machine-gun-like chatter which is directed at birds or other prey that are out of reach, often made when a cat is watching them through a window. Then there are grunts, snarls, growls, hisses and spitting, a short call of greeting: 'Welcome home!' and a variation which seems more interrogative: 'Well?' or 'Where've you been?' It does not require much skill to recognize them all. Frequently a vocal signal will be reinforced by gesture: a nudge to gain attention, a paw reaching out or a movement to the cupboard where food is stored or a

What has frightened this kitten that it has arched its back and raised its fur in a typical defensive posture?

Watch out – those backward-pointing ears suggest this cat is getting angry and the photographer should be on his guard!

door that the cat wants opened. Often the mimetic signals will be used without any voice at all. One very clear action is to scratch around a food bowl as though turning over litter, leaving no doubt at all as to what the cat thinks of that particular meal!

By rolling over on its side and presenting an exposed belly a cat or kitten may solicit play, from both other cats and humans, or courtship if it is a queen in season. This is the position in which its mother washed its underside and perhaps that is why many cats like having their bellies tickled when they roll back like this; however, be careful, for it is also a very deceptive position. Apparently so vulnerable, it also frees the cat's back legs so that they can kick out with raking claws to inflict quite serious injury.

Except when necessary to establish territorial or sexual dominance cats will usually avoid a fight: for them discretion is definitely the better part of valour. A confrontation will be extended for some time to establish submission and only token swipes made with the paws. Even if it goes beyond that fights between males will often be restricted to bites and clawing directed at the shoulder and neck where there is a thickening of the skin and they will do less damage.

The neck is where the hunting cat delivers its killing bite on rodents and birds. The lie of the fur or feathers seems to be a guide to its correct position, for a cat will sometimes move its nose along the body before striking, though on the pounce the restriction of the neck will be the main visual clue to locating the place. An experienced cat severs the spinal cord with its canine teeth but domestic cats not normally allowed out hunting may not have this knowledge, which appears to be acquired, not inherent, so that prey may be caught without being killed. A mouse or bird may be brought home as an offering, as a mother cat brings prey back to her kittens, and although you may wish to discourage your cat from doing this you should not be angry, the cat is behaving instinctively – and offering you a present! If the prey is unharmed release it out of the cat's sight and at a safe distance; if badly injured it is kindest to put it out of its misery. Some cats which have never been exposed to live prey as kittens ignore it but it is extremely difficult to train a cat not to catch things if it is allowed to go out where it can do so, partly because you must administer reproof when it actually does the catching, not when it brings the creature home.

Cats are instinctively predators and hunting is a natural part of their lives. They show great skill and patience in tracking down their prey. A cat may wait for hours beside a route it expects prey to take, hidden in cover and scarcely moving. It will creep slowly and stealthily to stalk its quarry, keeping its body as low as possible and its ears down, especially if peering over a barrier; moving swiftly but noiselessly

The seagull's beak is quite enough to keep this cat at bay. Cats often seem quite frightened by big birds, an instinctive reaction to aerial predators, perhaps.

through cover; finally breaking into a run when it deems the moment for attack has come or jumping down upon the prey from a vantage point above. Usually a cat will leap to the side of its victim and then make a final lunge so that, should there be resistance, it is firmly anchored on its back legs and stable in its attack.

Rodents and spiders seem to be the easiest things for cats to catch, only a few seem to be really good at catching birds, for this requires a different technique. The spring and final pounce would give a bird plenty of time to fly away so the strike must be made immediately, and the bird caught in the mouth or knocked down with a paw as it takes flight. Flies, butterflies and bees seem to be delicacies for many cats. A stung mouth or tongue can swell up and block the air passages and should rapidly be given treatment, but some cats seem impervious to stings. Another special technique is used by cats to scoop fish out of water, placing a paw below the fish and flipping it out on to the bank. It has been said that some cats use their tails like an angler's line, but there is no evidence to support this suggestion.

Above: This Siamese has eyes and ears focused on its prey and is keeping its body low, ready to rush forward and spring.

Right: All small rodents are among cats' prey and they can tackle animals as big as a rabbit, as well as birds, lizards, insects and even snakes.

On the other hand there are plenty of records of cats killing snakes – evidence of their skill and fast reactions and a reminder of their veneration in ancient Egypt.

Sometimes involvement in a fight or a narrow escape in an accident can have a traumatic effect upon a cat, leaving it in a state of shock, expressed in depression and lack of interest, perhaps with shivering and hypersensitivity to touch and a raising of the nictitating membrane over the eyes.

After catching small prey some cats play with it, sometimes letting a mouse go and catching it again or throwing it up into the air.

Cats are very much creatures of habit. They will have their own pattern for the day, places for washing (it happens almost everywhere, but proper grooming sessions may be more localized), places to lie in the sun, places from which to watch the world. They may have an accepted schedule of rights of way with other neighbourhood cats so that they do not have territorial confrontations. They will expect meals at regular times. They will wake you up and, especially if allowed to sleep in your bedroom or on the bed, may even let it be known that you have stayed up past the usual hour, as if to announce to visitors that it really is time that they went home. They will remind you if you attempt to leave the house without giving them breakfast, or that you have forgotten to make time for their regular game. Many will also be responsive to an owner's problems. They will sense illness, sorrow, frustration or depression and curl up with you to give emotional support – but if you look like losing your temper they will do their best to keep their distance.

The close attachment of some cats to their humans has been dramatically demonstrated by the difficulties which some have overcome to be reunited with them after separation. Although some cats become strays – either because they have rejected their homes, have been thrown out or badly treated or because some trauma has disoriented them – most have a very good sense of direction and of local topography. There are numerous records of cats finding their way home after being taken away by new owners or accidentally going on a trip – and cases of cats returning to an old locality even though their owners are no

Cats usually catch fish by flipping them out of the water on to the bank.

longer there. However, much more difficult to explain are the cases where a cat, left behind when its owner has moved, has turned up at the new family home, the location of which it cannot have known by any means that we understand – unless by some form of extra-sensory perception. There are instances, authenticated by individual characteristics such as old injuries, not just by appearance, of cats travelling thousands of miles over many months across unknown territory to find their humans: on one occasion from New York across the continent to California.

Such situations are exceptional, but the warmth of a cat's response to the care and affection that you give it will always be worth far more than the effort it demands. As a cat gets older it may need additional care, like any senior citizen. Some cats begin to show their age around nine years, but each individual will be different. Twelve years used to be considered a good age for a cat but with improved medical care they now can live much longer and cats of twenty years old are not so very uncommon.

An elderly cat will be more susceptible to disturbance and cold and will not have so much resistance to throw off infections. It will be less active so watch that it does not eat too much and become obese. Take it to the vet for a general check-up once a year, even if there has been no sign of illness. Elderly cats will like familiar places and things and should not be boarded out in a cattery unless they have been used to going there previously. If you move home make sure that they are given plenty of attention to help them to

Right: Cats wash places that they cannot reach with their tongues by wetting their paws and using them like a facecloth.

Below: The occasional scratch does not mean a cat has fleas. You probably scratch your head when you are thinking something over.